GW00995286

30
Most Conv
Cases of
Reincarnation

TRUTZ HARDO

JAICO PUBLISHING HOUSE

Ahmedabad Bangalore Chennai
Delhi Hyderabad Kolkata Mumbai

Published by Jaico Publishing House
A-2 Jash Chambers, 7-A Sir Phirozshah Mehta Road
Fort, Mumbai - 400 001
jaicopub@jaicobooks.com
www.jaicobooks.com

Published in arrangement with
Verlag "Die Silberschnur" GmbH
Steinstraße 1
D-56593 Güllesheim
Germany

To be sold only in India, Bangladesh, Bhutan,
Pakistan, Nepal, Sri Lanka and the Maldives.

30 MOST CONVINCING CASES OF REINCARNATION
ISBN 978-81-8495-910-9

First Jaico Impression: 2016

Printed by
Repro India Limited, Mumbai

CONTENTS

The knowledge of rebirth
is the turning point
in the history of mankind.
—Friedrich Nietzsche

INTRODUCTION

Dear readers, in your hands is a book which dares to suggest that after reading it you will no longer be the same person as you are now, at least as far as your outlook on life is concerned. At the end of the year 2000, reincarnation has finally been proven. The famous psychiatrist Professor Ian Stevenson M.D. has scientifically proven that reincarnation is a reality.

I will show you a number of case histories to substantiate this claim. Some of these have come from children and adults who remembered their past lives, later their memories having been proven to be accurate. Others were retrieved by means of regression techniques. In the fourth part of this book I will deal with some indisputable proofs which came to light in 1997 with the publication of Professor Stevenson's book Reincarnation and Biology – A contribution to the Etiology of Birth Defects. I will then

close my book with some thoughts on what the conse-
quences may be for the individual and for society as a whole,
when the concept of reincarnation becomes totally integrated
into our way of thinking.

The interest in reincarnation is growing, the latest demo-
graphic surveys continue to show a rising interest in
reincarnation. Professor Stevenson's book, including the
condensed version where Reincarnation and Biology intersect
will no doubt serve to push this interest even higher.

So from now on we can say with certainty that reincarnation
really exists. Even Jesus[1] and all the early Christians believed
in it. Today we no longer need to *believe* in it, since
reincarnation has been scientifically proven, just as the law
of gravity was proven some time ago. We are now able to
know that it is possible to return to earth repeatedly, and
that you dear readers have been here many times before.
What was until recently a belief for millions of people has
now been discovered to be the truth. The *intuitive feeling*, or
rather the *inner knowing* of reincarnation, has now shown itself
to be correct. One is no longer ridiculed for these beliefs.
On the contrary, people are beginning to ask questions,
wondering why they have always just believed, and are now
asking themselves how reincarnation really works in practice.

In the past people were simply told what they should believe.
To shake the existing belief systems that often dated back
hundreds or thousands of years was not permitted. Our

forefathers had been *believers,* so it was generally assumed that their beliefs were true. Otherwise how could so many generations have been totally mistaken? We spent generations regurgitating the beliefs others had fed us. Now through regression therapy we can reach our own inner source, which often presents us with something completely different than the traditional belief systems would have us believe. Our new awareness is based on that which is continually flowing from our inner source of knowing, and the old stagnant beliefs no longer satisfy our thirst for knowledge.

In the past we allowed ourselves to form our beliefs according to that what was poured in by the generally accepted opinion. Where our belief structures were concerned, we allowed ourselves to be led by whatever was fed us from outside. We absorbed these beliefs from outside and tried to convert them to an inner experience. This only worked to a certain extent. It was a rather limited way of looking at things. Now millions of *seekers* have discovered that the truth can be found inside themselves. We no longer search for the truth far and wide, but look to our inner depths to find it. In this way we have found a direct path to truth. Deep within us is hidden a large treasure of wisdom which in this new age can be tapped by each and every one of us. We no longer blindly follow belief systems like sheeps, but instead look inside taking full responsibility for all that we discover. One of the treasures which the knowledgeable and wise of all times discovered was that of reincarnation.

This was rejected by the main religions, which continued to spread across Europe. In the laws of reincarnation everyone has to become responsible for his or her own spiritual development, and the healing of his or her soul over many lifetimes. Seen in this light, highly organised institutions of belief become unnecessary, and are robbed of their power over the people. For this reason it is totally understandable why, for example, the Christian Church of the 13[th.] Century completely destroyed the Cathars in their gruesome crusade. The Cathars believed in reincarnation and had separated themselves from the Papacy, and were a threat to the ruling order. Many theologians watched with regret as their followers leapt off the *slow train* of Church beliefs and changed to the *Intercity Express* of a new era, in which reincarnation had become part of the regular *decor.* This is why many theologians are asking for modernisation of the *Church train,* so that this too can be equipped with the up-to-date décor, namely that of reincarnation. Maybe this train is also in need of a faster engine, in order to keep up with the *Express trains* of modern time.

In Brazil approximately 80% of the Catholic population believe in reincarnation. For them their belief in reincarnation does not conflict with their religion. Knowing this, the church elders are wise enough not to forbid the belief in reincarnation, since they would otherwise have empty churches. In fact, they endeavour to show the Pope the validity of reincarnation. The Pope responded by claiming that he is unable to do anything in this situation because more than 50% of his Cardinals still resist accepting reincarnation for what it is[2]. Why does he not put to use his wonder weapon *Ex Cathedra* in this case, and prescribe the belief in Reincarnation as it was in ancient Christian times, now only enriched by the latest findings of Reincarnation research? Or should Christianity wait until the aged Cardinals have passed away and new Cardinals have donned their hats? These are the thoughts of many modern theologians who have had a good look around the above-mentioned *Inter City Express*. I had occasionally the pleasure of meeting them at my regression seminars.

For those of you who are not convinced of reincarnation, and wish to stick with your convictions, I warn you against reading this book. If you still wish to read it, then be prepared that much may change in your outlook on life. Once more I warn you to close this book immediately, as it may influence you to such a degree that you will no longer be the same person you are now. You could find yourself in conflict with your religious beliefs. Surely you would not want this? If on the other hand your thinking tends more towards the scientific, then you could also find yourself in conflict with these views. Surely you do not want this either? I am sure you also would not want to challenge the great leaders such as Marx, Freud, and Heidegger? This literature could be a spiritual dynamite for you. So, quickly put this book away! For here at last is the indisputable proof that us humans have many lives and that our present life is just one link in a whole chain of past lives. Once this idea has been totally accepted there will be a complete revolution in our way of thinking about the world and ourselves. For me there is no doubt that this will occur, since the truth invariably comes to light!

1

CHILDREN'S MEMORIES OF PAST LIVES

THE BOY WHO ONCE AGAIN LIVES WITH HIS WIFE FROM THE PAST

I shall begin with a story which Tag Powell, an American friend, leader of seminars and publisher of various books confided in me during a annual book fair in Frankfurt.

"Do you know something Tom?" (This is what my friends call me)."I can tell you about a case of reincarnation that is so extraordinary that it could surely turn every sceptic into a dedicated follower of reincarnation. Even so, I am not inclined to give away the names of the respective couple and their son. I am sure you know this couple, at least by name, since he is a famous author, and he and his wife run seminars in the whole of America." I would have loved to know the name of this couple, but I was not going to encourage Tag to break his promise to them. Even so I asked, "Does he run courses on spiritual themes like Reincarnation,

Astrology or...?" "No, no!" Interrupted Tag, "he's a bloody scientist and one of his books has become a national best seller. He is owner of many patents. His wife is also a scientist and an author."

The couple in question had a son whom I shall call Michael. When he was a baby he desperately wanted to hold his father's Rolex watch in his hands. He kept reaching for it again and again. As soon as he could speak his first words, he pointed to the watch and said, "Mine!" One day, when his parents called him by his name, he pointed to himself and said, "Sunny." He insisted so long and so forcefully on being called Sunny that his parents soon gave in and agreed to his wishes. A few months later the young nipper said, "Me Sunny Ray."

His mother was immediately taken by this name, which after all meant sunray. So from now on she called him *My Little Sunray*. One day he told them that he had a wife whose name was Dawn, and that they had both lived in Texas. In his present parent's house they mainly listened to classical music. When the radio played a Country and Western song Michael would sing along, and to their amazement he even seemed to know the words. One day Michael was looking at a book about dogs with his mother. All of a sudden he pointed to a white spaniel and called out excitedly, "That's my dog Willie!" His parents never seemed to seriously consider that their son could be talking about something from a previous life.

Some time later when the boy was seven years old, the couple was running a seminar in Texas. One of the people taking part was Dawn Ray. During a break Michael's father started a conversation with the woman, and asked her whether she was married. She told him, "I have been a widow for eight years." "What was your husband's first name?" "Sunny", she replied. The couple then looked at each other in amazement. Then he asked the woman whether she would please come to their hotel after the seminar because they had something important to tell her. When she got there they told her that they have a son who claims to have been married to someone called Dawn Ray from Texas in a previous life. "Did you own a white spaniel?" asked Michael's mother. "Oh yes, that was our Willie. He and Sunny were inseparable!" Mrs. Ray now was determined to get to know Michael. Michael's parents phoned home to arrange a flight for him and two days later the seven-year-old was able to fly out to be with them. They did not tell their son over the phone why it was so important for him to come to Texas so suddenly. After collecting him from the airport they took him straight away to Mrs. Ray's house. When she opened the door, the boy recognised her immediately and called out excitedly, "Dawn!" He stretched out his hands and ran into the arms of the dazed Mrs. Ray, hugged her and gave her a big kiss on the cheek.

Finally everyone sat down in the living room. Mrs. Ray, who was still sceptical, asked Michael whether he knew this house. He did not recognise it. On hearing that, she explained that she only moved into this house two years after the death of Sunny. Then Michael asked her whether she had kept his guitar. Mrs. Ray was highly amazed at this question. She went to a cupboard and took out a guitar and placed it into the outstretched hands of the little man. Michael held the instrument like a competent guitar player. After a couple of tries, even though the fret board was not the right size for a seven-year-old, he began to play and sing a well-known folk song. This especially amazed his parents, since to their knowledge their son had never played the guitar. Then he asked Mrs. Ray, whom he now addressed as Dawn, whether she also kept his watch for him. She fetched a box in which the watch was kept. It was a Rolex identical to the one his father was wearing. Then he asked her for his camera. His parents first wanted to know exactly what it looked like. When he had described it, Dawn fetched it and it perfectly matched his description. Also his pipe, which he wanted to see, had first to be described by him.

Tag closed his reports with the comment, "I would have loved to have been witness to that evening." "Me too," I agreed. "Gosh Tag! That's really an incredible story!" "The best bit is yet to come," he continued. "Dawn sold her house and moved in with the family in California. She looked after Michael, since his parents were often away travelling. When she moved to New York Michael missed her so much that even though he was only fourteen-years-old his parents agreed to let him live in New York with her. They have lived together ever since." "If these events were really like you say or even close to it, then this is a real classic!" I said. "Honest to God, this is a true story."[3]

Dear readers, my jaw dropped in amazement when I heard this story. Perhaps it was the same for you. One more word for our dear sceptics who are in no way inclined to believe in reincarnation, but who still read this report, you still have the chance to put this book down. For if you do not you may find yourselves having to agree that maybe there really is some truth in it. To the rest of my readers I would now like to report on some more unquestionable cases.

BORN AGAIN TO THE SAME PARENTS — THIS TIME AS TWINS

On the 5th May 1957, while playing on the pavement, eleven-year-old Joanna and her six-year-old sister Jacqueline Pollock were run down by a car. The woman driver had been semi-conscious due to drug abuse. Although the parent's sadness was great, they pardoned the guilty driver and wrote a letter to her.[4]

When Mrs. Pollock was pregnant a year later, her husband revealed to her that he had a vision. He saw that she would give birth to twin girls and that these two would be their two lost daughters reborn. Even though Mrs. Pollock was reassured by a gynaecologist that there was only one audible heartbeat present and not twins, Mr. Pollock was still convinced that his *knowing* was correct. Later he was proven to be right. On the 4th October 1958, Mrs. Pollock gave birth to identical girl twins. The first child was given the name Gillian; the second born ten minutes later was named Jennifer.

While their father was admiring his new daughters, he noticed a scar above the right eyebrow of Jennifer, the younger of the two girls. His recently deceased daughter Jacqueline had had the same scar in exactly the same place. She had fallen at about the age of three, and a visible scar had remained on her forehead. To his amazement he also discovered a brown birthmark the size of his thumb on Jennifer. His daughter Jacqueline had had exactly the same birthmark in the same place. All this proved to him that his earlier vision that he had received was true. Gillian and Jennifer were truly his first daughters reborn. Mrs. Pollock, being a strict Catholic, still rejected the idea of reincarnation until the following events occurred.

When the twins were four months old the Pollocks moved to a different area, only to return to Hexham on a visit two and-a-half years later. To the amazement of the parents, their two daughters knew their way around this area extremely well. Without being able to see the school, since it was hidden from sight by the church, one of the girls said, "The school is just around the corner." The other one pointed to a hill and said, "Our playground was behind there. It had a slide and a swing." When they approached their old house the two sisters recognised it immediately. Even so, Mrs. Pollock, unlike her husband, still did not want to believe that the twins were really her recently deceased daughters reborn.

When the twins were four years old, Mr. Pollock opened a box, which had been closed for over three years. In it had been kept the toys of his first children. He placed some of these outside the twins' bedroom door, as he wanted to see whether they would recognise their toys from the past. When the girls came out of their room – where their mother stood as witness to their reactions – Jennifer picked up the first doll and said, "Oh! That's Mary. (And picking up the second doll,) that's my Suzanne! I haven't seen them for ages." She used the same names, which Jacqueline had previously given her two dolls. "Father Christmas gave us these a long time ago." She turned to Gillian, and pointing to another toy she said, "And that's your washing machine." Now Mrs. Pollock was finally convinced that her twins really were her first daughters, and that her Church must be mistaken in refuting reincarnation.

Both the children developed over-cautious responses when crossing roads and feared speeding cars. The older daughter Gillian loved to comb peoples' hair, especially her father's. This interest had been the same in their fatally injured Joanna. Joanna had been five years older than her sister Jacqueline, and the sisters had spent most of their time holding hands and had seemed inseparable. Jacqueline always listened to her older sister; whatever she said was right for her. The same behaviour surfaced once again in the twins. The one born ten minutes later leaves all the decisions to her sister and does what she tells her. Once again both of them loved walking around hand in hand, and as before one never seemed to want to do anything different than the other[5].

If you had daughters like this, would you not be equally convinced of reincarnation, as was Mrs. Pollock, even if you followed a strict religious belief? There are thousands of cases that show us the same or very similar circumstances to those described here. We will look at some of these more closely later on. Sadly, most parents forbid their children to talk about such things. What their children say may well go against their beliefs, and often they are also concerned about what the neighbours may think if they got to hear about it. In India the belief in reincarnation is widely spread. One is able to speak freely to others about who one was and what one has experienced in the past. Still many parents forbid their children to mention their memories of past lives. Their unfounded fear is often that children who remember past lives may die young, or may become homesick for their previous family and may wish to be reunited with them.

Even before Professor Stevenson began his scientific research into reincarnation, there was a case of someone in India in the 1930's who remembered a past life, knowledge of which soon spread beyond the borders of India. News about this case spread through magazines containing paranormal reports, as well as by word of mouth. The case was that of Shanti Devi.

A MOTHER HUGS HER SON WHO IS OLDER THAN SHE IS

Shanti Devi was born in Delhi on 11th December 1926. She was not very talkative as a child. At the age of three she began to speak of her home being in Mathura, a town between New Delhi and Agra. When she was four years old she began to speak more about her earlier life and about having been married. She had lived in a household with her sisters, her mother and her husband. Shanti told her mother that she came from a more well to do home and that this present house was not her home. She said, "You are not my real mother. You don't even look like her." Furthermore she told her that her husband used to have a fabric shop, and that her house in Mathura was painted yellow. Her parents did not want to believe any of it.

One day she refused to eat the food that was put on the table. When asked why she didn't want to eat it she said, "I want *Satva* food." "*Satva* food? No one here has ever used this expression." Shanti replied, "We use that word in Mutra (Mathura), we don't eat meat. It is not right to eat animals. It is a terrible crime. Still some people eat meat, but we don't." When her mother asked her whom she meant by *we*, four-year-old Shanti answered that she meant her husband's family. "I personally see to it that my husband only eats *Satva* food. Even our servants are not permitted to prepare his food. When he returns home from his shop by the *Dvarkad Temple*, I serve him his dinner. He likes things to be that way." After that incident, her father was very understanding and allowed his daughter to eat vegetarian dishes.

After dinner, when their daughter had left the room, Mrs. Bahadur said to her husband, "What on earth did we do in our previous life, to be experiencing such bad karma now, by being punished with a mentally ill daughter?" Her husband answered, "If it is true that she remembers her past life, then she has some bad luck awaiting her. Even the old scriptures speak of this. "With this comment he was referring to the *Vedic Scriptures* in which it is written that a child that remembers past lives would die young. To avoid this, Mr. Bahadur and his wife forbade their daughter to talk about her former life in Mathura, hoping she would soon lose her memories and so stop talking about them.

Shanti nonetheless went on speaking of her past life, even to visitors who came to their house, She hoped that at least one of them would believe her, and help her fulfil her wish to go to Mathura. At school she regularly referred to her past life by making comments to her friends and teachers. Her classmates teased her about being married and having a son. Her class teacher, who was related to the Bahadur family, showed an interest in her case and questioned her about it. He even asked her for the name of her previous husband. She just answered, "I will recognise him when I see him." (It was not permitted for a Hindu woman to use her husband's name.) When her teacher finally promised her that he would take her to Mathura if she told him his name, she said, "My husband's name is Pandit Kedernath Chobey. " After she had given him the complete address, he told his friend who was the head of the school, and together they wrote a letter to that address in the vain hope of receiving a reply. The letter said:

Dear Sir,

I have recently got to know a girl by the name of Shanti Devi. She is a resident in a part of the town called Chirakhana. She is the daughter of a businessman called Rang Bahadur Mathur. She is nearly nine years old. She is able to tell us amazing details about you. She claims the following to be true: "In my past life I belonged to the Chobey family from Mathura. I belonged to the Brahman caste and my husband's name was Kedernath. He was the owner of a shop near the *Dvarkad Temple.* My house was painted completely yellow. My name was Lugdi Devi."

May I bother you dear Pandit, and ask you kindly to inform me whether there is any truth in these claims.

Did Lugdi Devi exist? Please let me know whether there was really such a person.

May God bless you.
With the greatest respect,
Your,
Lala Kishan Chaud.
Director of the Ranija School, Daryganj, Delhi.

A few weeks later the two teachers held a reply from this person in their hands. They were truly amazed at what was written in the letter:

Lala Kishan Chaud, director of the Ranija School, Daryganj, Delhi,

I was very surprised and somewhat excited when I read your letter. The things you wrote about are absolutely correct. I had a wife called Lugdi Devi. She has since died. I really do have a shop near the *Dvarkad Temple.* Who is this girl who knows all this?

Mr. Chobey was extremely keen to find out whether this girl was really his deceased wife reborn. He asked his cousin to look up Shanti Devi's parents in the city in order to find out more about their daughter, and to put Shantis' memories of their previous life together to the test. When this cousin met Shanti face to face she immediately recognised him as one of her husband's younger cousins and called him by name. Shanti then asked him about her son Nabanita Lall and inquired about his well-being. She described the layout of her house and its location, which was directly in front of the *Dvarkad Temple*. Her previous husband's cousin was so convinced by her exact descriptions that he did not bother to write to Chobey about his impressions as previously arranged, but immediately travelled to him to tell him that Shanti Devi really was his wife from past life.

Mr. Chobey, whose curiosity had now been awakened by his cousin, decided to travel to Delhi with his present wife, his son from his first marriage and his cousin, in order to see this girl with his own eyes. When they arrived, Shanti was at school. They decided to pretend that Chobey was an older brother when meeting Shanti's family. With this he wanted to put Shanti to the test once more, and to make sure that her family would not tell her before they met; after all they did not really know who was coming to visit. When the eight-year-old came home from school they told her that she has a visitor waiting for her in the other room.

When she entered the room she immediately recognised her husband from the past. Without saying a word she bowed her head in shy respect before him and stood by his side, as was the custom for Hindu wives in the presence of their husbands. Her eyes were gleaming with joy. They asked her why she behaved like this since the man at her side was Chobey's older brother. Shanti replied calmly, "No he's not, he is my husband. I have told you about him many times." When she looked at the ten-year-old boy she immediately knew him to be her son. She hugged him and cried for a long time. Then she asked her mother to bring all her own toys so that she could give them to her son Nabanita. When her mother showed reluctance she ran off herself and returned minutes later with an armful of toys. Even though she was more than a year younger than Nabanita, everyone could detect a motherly love in the way she looked at him and behaved towards him. Shanti was so moved by everything that she often had to cry, and infected everyone present with her tears. It was not long before the news of this extraordinary family re-union had spread throughout the neighbourhood. In no time at all a large number of interested people had appeared.

Mr. Chobey suggested that they escape the bustle in an open horse drawn cart. During their walk Shanti and Nabanita walked hand in hand. Later when they return-ed, Shanti begged her mother to prepare a meal of all her husband's favourite dishes. She also recognised her jewellery from her past life, which Mr. Chobey's new wife was now wearing. After their meal she asked her husband why he had remarried, "Did we not agree that

after the death of one of us neither would remarry?"
Mr. Chobey had apparently gazed at the floor feeling
uncomfortable, according to Shanti's father who later
confided this to the journalist Jeffrey Iverson. Shanti's
father encouraged Shanti to tell him more about her
house. To this Shanti replied, "There is a courtyard in
the centre of the house. That's where the well is. I often
used to sit on the edge of it to bathe." Many other
questions were put to her concerning her family in this
past life. Mr. Chobey asked Shanti how she recognised
her son immediately, since on the day she died he was
only nine days old. Shanti's spontaneous reply, like that
of a wise woman, was, "He is my life, the life in me
recognised the life in him." Mr. Chobey excused
himself, since he wished to discuss some private
matters with Shanti. When they finally returned to the
others, he announced, "No one other than my previous
wife and myself could know all these things. This girl
is my deceased wife Lugdi. I am no longer in any doubt
about it."[6]

My dear readers, could you continue to have the slightest
doubt about the validity of these experiences? A hardened
critic will still doubt everything that does not fit his view
of life, no matter how convincing it may sound. To be critical
a good thing, as long as you are prepared to look into the
issue in depth and then decide, without prejudice, what you
can or cannot accept. Such an unprejudiced critic should
also have the courage to look at the truth, and once he has

found something to be true, to admit this to himself. Our story about Shanti Devi is not yet complete.

News of these events spread like wildfire. The paper "Indian Press" sent out its reporters, making it possible for millions of readers to hear about this latest sensation. Mr. Bahadur was now encouraged by various parties to finally fulfil Shanti Devi's wish to travel to Mathura. Mr. and Mrs. Bahadur absolutely forbade this out of fear of losing their daughter to her past family. Mahatma Gandhi showed great interest in this case of a young girl remembering her past life, so he personally decided to go and meet Shanti. His visit was primarily in order to personally ask her all sorts of questions, and secondly to ask her parents to allow their daughter to travel to Mathura. This wish from such an illustrious man, whom the Indians have worshipped like a god for generations, could not be refused.

Finally a committee was formed to investigate this case scientifically, which consisted of fifteen people chosen honorary among them was a publisher of one of the most popular newspapers, a solicitor and a parliamentary backbencher. They decided to accompany Shanti Devi to Mathura in order to examine her claims there and then. She had never been there before and her father also reassured her emphatically that he himself has never been to Mathura either. On November 24th 1935, twelve days after Mr. Chobey had visited Shanti Devi, her parents and the entire committee boarded the train that was to take them on the three-hour journey to Mathura. While on the train someone mentioned the time, and the nine-year-old announced that precisely at this time the gates to the *Dvarkad Temple* were being closed. Instead of using the word gate in her Hindi language, she used an unusual word only commonly used in Mathura and it's surrounding area.

When they arrived at their destination, thousands of onlookers informed about the imminent arrival of Shanti Devi by their newspapers had gathered at the station. A tall man wearing a turban and carrying a stick pushed his way through the crowd, stood in front of the girl and said, "Do you know me?" Shanti bowed down with respect and touched his feet. Then she rose and stood by his side. She turned to one of the committee members and said, "This is my husband's oldest brother." When they drove through the streets in an open horse-drawn carriage, she could tell which roads had not been surfaced in the past and could point out the houses that had not been there before. When they arrived at a crossing, she climbed down from the carriage and led the committee to her house that was surrounded by a huge crowd of people. An elderly man was waiting there dressed in Brahmin clothing. She bowed down before him and said, "This is my father-in-law." Among the crowd she also discovered her twenty-five-year-old brother and her father in law's brother from her past life.

To her amazement the house was not yellow as she remembered it. She was then told that after her death the house had changed hands, and that the new owners had painted it a different colour. When she was led through the house and was pointing out all the things that had changed one of the people present asked her whether she knew where the "Jajarie Khann" was. This word is only used in this area and so would be unfamiliar to the girl from Delhi. She immediately went downstairs and pointed to the toilet.

In the afternoon, one of the committee members took Shanti on his shoulders to avoid the crush of the crowds, for her job now was to find the other house in which she had also lived with her husband. Following her directions she was carried to a building. She pointed to it and said, "That is my house!" She led the committee into the house. First they came to a yard situated in the centre of the house. Once there, she was shocked not to find the well in which she used to bathe. She pointed to a particular place and said that the well used to be there. They lifted a stone slab off the ground and found under it the well she had spoken of. After that, she led the committee through the house and described all the rooms in great detail. When they reached the bedroom she pointed to the floor and said, "This is where I hid my money. If you check here under the floor you will find a box containing 150 Rupees." They lifted the floorboards in the presence of Mr. Chobey, her previous husband, and found the box as described. But there was no money in it. Shanti was extremely surprised and said that someone must have taken it. Mr. Chobey now owned up to having taken the 150 Rupees out of the box after her death.

After this incident Shanti led the committee to the river Jumna to show them where she used to bathe. She pointed to a house and said, "My parents used to live in that house." Then she suddenly ran off in the direction of the house and the committee had to be quick to catch up with her. In the house there were forty-five people. Among them she recognised her mother from the past and immediately went to sit on her lap. The older woman asked the girl whether she could tell her about something that they both knew about from their past. Shanti reminded her that she had promised her on her deathbed that she would bring flowers and sweets to her for Lord Krishna. When the nine-year-old asked her whether she had kept this promise, her mother from the past had to admit to having forgotten about it. Then Shanti said with regret, "Why has no one kept their promises? Why do people always lie to the dying?" The woman now totally convinced by having publicly discussed the experiences she had shared with the girl in their past hugged her more intimately than ever. She was certain that this girl really was her daughter Lugdi. Suddenly the tears flowed and Shanti now greeted her father from the past, he too was touched and began to cry. The remaining people present were also moved to tears.

Shanti's present day parents had also accompanied their

daughter to Mathura and were witness to this moving scene. Mrs. Bahadur was in turmoil, since she was certain that her daughter would no longer wish to return to Delhi with her. She had found her previous mother and they were now hugging each other as though they would never again wish to be separated. Mrs. Bahadur turned to her husband in despair and said, "They want to rob us of our daughter. They are all part of this conspiracy." Shanti's previous mother sensed their fear and despair and said, "Let Shanti decide. Only she has the right to decide which family she wishes to live with." Mr. Bahadur, who had innately let go of his daughter, tried to comfort his wife by saying, "It is fate my dear, it is Karma. We are all subject to this law."

Everyone now gathered in the room and looked at Shanti with great anticipation, wondering what her decision would be. Meantime she had gathered her thoughts and wiped her tears. She freed herself from the arms of her previous mother and whispered to her and her father, "Forgive me mother Jagti and father Chaturbhuj," and then walked out through the door. Meanwhile the news of these events had spread far and wide. Everyone who heard about it wanted to see this girl. This made getting back to the station rather difficult.

Imagine, dear readers, hearing of something like this happening in your immediate neighbourhood. What would you have done? Would you have stayed at home telling yourself, "There are bound to be reporters at the scene, and they will find out whether there's anything in this. I'm sure to read about it in tomorrow's newspapers." How the reporter writes about the event always defines our judgement of it. Please imagine that the reporter in question had a boss, who from the start considered reincarnation and all that to be utter nonsense, and who would put his energy into opposing it. How then would this newspaper report have turned out? What opinion would you then be able to form in your mind? Would it have been an objective view? Sadly reporters are often unable to recount the events the way they perceived and experienced them at the time. They too are subject to the guidelines laid down by their newspaper bosses. The bosses decide what to feed their readers and what should be conveyed as the truth. If a reporter does not keep to these rules, he is first warned and then if he continues to ignore the guidelines he is sacked. I know several journalists who are firm believers in reincarnation who have to hide their conviction, not daring to write about it, unless of course they worked for the popular press. These seem happy to embrace these kind of issues, since many readers know that there is more to life than schoolteachers would have us believe. Do you still wish to read more about Shanti Devi? I will presume you do.

Five years later, an inquisitive scientist decided to reopen the case of Shanti Devi, who by now had become famous in India. He wished to research her case in more depth. Dr. Bose looked up Shanti's previous husband to find out what he discussed with the girl on his first visit after retiring to

another room with her. Dr. Bose had reassured him that as
a scientist he was curious to find out the truth about
everything, including things like the intimate discussions
with Shanti. Was it not Mr. Chobey who announced that
he no longer doubted the validity of Shanti's statements?
Mr. Chobey told him that to this day he has not wanted to
talk to anyone else about these private discussions. Mr. Bose
was to be the first person with whom he would be pleased
to discuss the matter. He told him that he had asked Shanti
to tell him about things that only she and he himself knew
about. Shanti then suggested his present wife leave the
room. He replied saying that she may speak freely in her
presence. She then answered, "Ask me what you wish to know
and I will answer everything." He reminded her about an
accident that had caused her a lot of pain at the time. Shanti
described the events in detail and could show him the exact
place on her body where she had injured herself during a
fall. These exact descriptions had completely convinced him
of the truth of her claims.

Dr. Bose himself went to visit Shanti, who by now was quite
older. He wanted to hear about the whole sequence of events
surrounding her accident in her own words. As always she
could remember everything clearly. Dr. Bose asked her, "Can
you remember how you died and what you experienced after
that?" At this point I became a little cautious as an author
whether or not to repeat this conversation to anyone,
knowing that for many of you these truths about life after
death would be completely new. I assure you that I myself

have heard of such reports from hundreds of people whom I guided back to their previous lives, and whom I gave the opportunity to relive their physical deaths. In most cases I have no doubt about the validity of their experiences. Shanti described to Dr. Bose what she experienced during and after her death.

Shortly before her death she found herself surrounded by darkness. In the darkness she discovered a shining light above her. In a state, which could only be described as cloud-like, she had floated towards the light. She was no longer aware of her earthly body on the bed and therefore did not turn around to look at it. She no longer felt any pain. She found herself standing in the bright light. She could see four figures in yellow robes approaching her. They led her into a beautiful garden the likes of which she had never seen on earth. Her own comment about this was, "It was more beautiful than I could describe with words." The beings there appeared to be holy. They were of both sexes. She was told many things; for example the place where she now was there was no darkness and therefore no night exists, only light. She was told that we are all the same beings, so it makes no difference whether someone was Hindu, Muslim or Christian. After having spent a long time in this other world, she was told that she was to return to earth, and was to be born again as a girl in Delhi. She was also told the name of the father whose daughter she would be. She experienced the descent to earth as a path leading back into the darkness. When the somewhat sceptical Dr. Bose asked the thirteen-year-old how she imagined it possible to see things without her five ordinary bodily senses after death, she answered that it was very difficult for her to explain to him exactly what she had experienced. She did tell him that without her physical body it was possible for her to see through walls, in other words, she could perceive things, which normally she was unable to see with her physical eyes. Apparently this experience was similar with all the senses.

It was only through the research of pioneers such as Dr. Elizabeth Kubler-Ross and Raymond Moody in the seventies that we got to hear of experiences which people had while clinically dead. This is to say, in a state where no heartbeat is felt and brain wave activity is no longer registered. These experiences and those of Shanti Devi who spoke of them over 40 years ago seemed to be the same.

Shanti Devi died in 1988. Because of her vows she made to her husband during her life as Lugdi, she never remarried. She was convinced that with this incarnation as Shanti Devi she had completed her earthly lives and would no longer have to return to earth. Professor Stephenson sees this particular case as a classic example in favour of reincarnation. The statements that Shanti Devi had made before her visit to Mathura have been documented by witnesses and proven to be correct. It was only afterwards that the details were double-checked at the place itself. It had not been possible for Shanti Devi to find out anything about what sort of person her previous husband had been, nor about the place where he had lived. Her father had also never been to Mathura before. This has to be a very convincing case in favour of reincarnation.

Surely the American professor must have wished for the case of Shanti Devi to have occurred during the time when he was carrying out his research. He would certainly have researched every possible detail, using all his scientific means available. Instead he had the task of researching over 2500 cases and in his book he describes over 70 of them in detail. Most of these were from children who claimed to have lived before. During his life he travelled thousands of miles in order to investigate many cases that could possibly be linked to reincarnation.

In Brazil he heard of a case in which the dying person told someone else that she wanted to be reborn as her child. This wish then came about. I perceive that these wishes we make relating to a future life on earth frequently do come true. When taking people back through regression I have helped hundreds of them to relive their last moments before death. It is in these moments that the dying often seem to programme their next life on earth, either with thoughts or spoken words.

I WISH TO BE REBORN
AS YOUR DAUGHTER

Maria Januaria Oliviero was the daughter of a wealthy Earl and landowner in south Brazil. Her friends called her Sinha (pronounced Sinja). Her friend Ida lived in far simpler conditions than she did. She was the wife of Mr. Lorenz, originally from German and now a schoolteacher in this area. Their homes were approximately 20 kilometres apart. In 1918 when Sinha was 28, she fell ill with tuberculosis, which in those days was a practically incurable disease. On her deathbed she told her friend Ida that she wished to be reborn as her daughter and informed her that, "When I return as your daughter I will tell you about the secret of rebirth. I will then tell you many things about my present life so that you will know the truth of it for yourself."[7]

Ten months later Ida Lorenz gave birth to a healthy daughter who was given the name Marta. When she was still very young and could only speak a few words, the landowner Mr. de Oliviero, accompanied by another man, came to visit the Lorenz family for a short while. Even though the man, who accompanied Mr. de Oliviero addressed the child in a friendly manner, she turned from him and immediately ran up to Mr. de Oliviero hugged him, lovingly stroked his beard and called him *Papa*.

When Marta was about two-and-a-half years old she asked her older sister Lola to carry her. When she refused the little girl said, "When I was big and you were little I often carried you." "When were you big?" asked her sister in return. "I didn't live here then. I lived far away from here where there were cows, oxen, oranges and goats which weren't really goat's." (She meant sheep but didn't know the right word.) When Lola told her parents about the things her younger sister had told her they were surprised, but put these statements down to imagination. They had not told their children anything about Sinha's intension of being reborn to them as their daughter.

After this, Lorenz carried out his own investigation into his youngest daughter's past. He told her he had never lived anywhere where there were 'goat's which were not goat's', to which the little girl replied, "Well, I had different parents in those days." One of her sisters jokingly asked whether she used to have a black servant girl like the one they now have. Marta then told her that she used to have a male black servant, a female black cook and a black servant boy. One day the boy was beaten by her father for forgetting to fetch water. Her father interrupted her saying, "But I have never beaten a black boy." "It was my other father who hit him," the little girl added quickly. "The black boy begged me saying, "Sinhazinha help me!" I begged my father not to hit him. He let him go and the boy ran away to fetch water." Her father inquired further, "Did he fetch the water from a stream?" "No, no," explained the girl, "there was no stream only a spring." Her father who knew what the de Olivieros family was like, knew that these statements were true. He then wanted to know who this Sinha or Sinhazinha was, (pronounced Sinjazinja, a shortened version of the first name, which means white cat.) "That was me. I also had another name. I was called Maria. I even had another name which I've forgotten now."

As you can see, we are not dealing with Marta mind reading, since Mr. Lorenz did not know Maria's full name. He also remembered nothing of the beatings that Mr. de Oliviero had dealt the coloured boy, but Maria's father later confirmed this fact. In the light of this evidence we seem to be dealing with a genuine case of reincarnation.

Mr. Lorenz now began to write down all statements and information relating to Marta's past life. It was only a matter of time before he had noted down 120 such pieces of information using German shorthand. Sadly someone in his family decided they were worthless pieces of paper and threw them away. Had this information been kept we would be dealing with one of the most thoroughly documented cases of a child's past life memories. Mr. Lorenz later tried to write down some of these statements from memory. Much of what Marta talked about was new to the Lorenz family, since they rarely got to hear much about the relationships and events taking place at Sinha's house.

One day Mrs. Lorenz asked her youngest daughter how she had welcomed her when she visited her as Sinha. Marta replied that she used to put the gramophone on just to please her. Only Mrs. Lorenz could have known of this incident since she had not talked to anyone else in the family about it. Another day when a woman belonging to her past family came to visit, the girl recognised her immediately calling her by her name. When the woman was then told that Marta was her recently deceased Aunt Maria she asked the girl, "If you were really Sinha, tell me how we were related to each other." Marta then told her that she had been her cousin and also her Godchild.

Marta begged her parents to take her to visit her father. When she was 12 years old she was finally granted her wish. It was only on this occasion that Mr. De Oliviero discovered that the Lorenz's youngest daughter was in fact his daughter Maria reborn. Finally he was completely convinced of this fact when he saw Marta going through the house making comments about all the changes, and stopping in front of a wall clock saying, "This used to be my clock. My name is engraved on the back in gold letters." Later they took the clock down and to their amazement they found the name Maria Januaria de Oliviero on the back in gold letters.

Even though Marta had been 12 years old when she remembered those details in Mr. de Oliviero's house, her memories of her past life as Maria had gradually begun to dry up from the age of seven onwards. When Professor Stevenson visited the now married Marta in Porto Allegre in 1962, she had apparently forgotten many things from her past life. None the less she was able to tell him the exact details of her last months as Maria, especially concerning the events surrounding her illness. This was of particular interest to him since he was a doctor.

When Marta had grown up, some of the older people who had known Maria noticed how similar the two were, even their handwriting was almost identical. Maria had died of tuberculosis as well as severe throat problems, and Marta seemed to have inherited these for the pain in her larynx was often so bad that even as a child she sometimes spoke with a very hoarse voice, or lost it altogether.

When Stevenson looked her up once more in 1972, in order to collect more evidence for his research, he was amazed how many details were still surfacing from her subconscious. For example, Maria's teacher, whom she had fallen in love with and had wanted to marry, had taken his own life after Maria's father had refused to consent to their marriage out of pure snobbery.

Even as a young girl Marta knew that one-day this beloved teacher named Florzinho would be reborn to her as her child. She did in fact bear two sons, but they both died shortly after birth. She is convinced that she gave birth to Florzinho twice in a row, because both babies had the same birthmarks in exactly the same place on their heads as her beloved Florzinho once had.

We will later explore the meaning of birthmarks and especially congenital deformities, since these revealed some of the most convincing evidence of reincarnation. But now

I wish to draw your attention to a case in which an unborn soul announces its wish to be reborn to a particular woman, telling her that she would recognise him by his scars. Professor Stevenson examined this case, which took place in South Eastern Alaska.

I WILL RETURN AS YOUR NEXT SON

The case of the Indian boy Corliss is one of my favourites to discuss during my lectures on reincarnation, since it has many interesting aspects to it. This boy belonged to a tribe of Tlingit Indians, of whom approximately 7000 still live in their original region of South Eastern Alaska. The belief in reincarnation is widely accepted in that region, as is the case among many Indians and Eskimo tribes; *belief* having become *knowing*.

Victor Vincent was a Tlingit fisherman. During the years before his death he visited his niece Corliss Chotkin Sen more and more frequently. She was the daughter of his sister, Gertrude. He seemed to be very fond of his niece and especially their youngest daughter whom he believed to be the reincarnation of his sister Gertrude. In other words, the daughter was her own grandmother, who had been Victor Vincent's sister.

About a year before his death Victor told his niece the following, "I will return as your next son. I hope I won't be stuttering as much then as I do now. Your son will bear these scars. He lifted his shirt to reveal a scar on his back, which had remained visible years after having had an operation. There were also needle marks clearly visible around this scar. Then Victor pointed to another scar from an operation, which he had on his nose. He said that this too would identify him in his next life as her son. He also told his niece why he wants to be reborn to her. "I know that with you I will be well looked after. You won't go off getting drunk." Sadly there were many alcoholics among his relations for alcohol had become a curse among his people. In many ways modern living had separated them from their traditions or brought them into conflict with them. On my travels around the world I have experienced many such examples of devastation where modern influences have had disastrous effects on indigenous people.

Eighteen months after Victor's death, Chotkin Sen gave birth to a boy, who was given his father's name Corliss Chotkin junior. His parents were convinced that their son was Uncle Victor reborn, since he was born with exactly those scars he had shown them before his death, namely on his nose and back.

When he was 13 months old his mother tried to help him pronounce his name Corliss. The boy suddenly pointed to himself saying, "Me Kahkody!" This had been the name of Vincent's tribe. Since he corrected every one who called him Corliss with the name Kahkody, this name finally stuck. When an aunt visited his mother and was told about Corliss being Vincent reborn, the woman said, "I knew it. After his death Victor appeared to me in a dream and said that he was now incarnating in your body so that he could be your son." The mother had waited in vain for such a dream since it was very common among them for the souls seeking to reincarnate to announce their arrival in a dream.

When Corliss was two years old he travelled to the neighbouring seaside town with his mother. Unexpectedly they met a young woman, and before any words were exchanged the little boy called out her name. He was so happy he jumped with joy calling her by her Tlingit name. For this woman had been his stepdaughter in his previous life. A little later the boy caught sight of a man among the pedestrians, pointed at him and said to his mother, "There's my son William."

A year later Mrs. Chotkin took her son along to a big Tlingit gathering. Among the many people present he saw an elderly woman and said, "That's the old dame. That's my Rose." This woman had been his previous wife, whom he used to call 'old dame' when he was Victor. In the years that followed Corliss recognised several of Victor's relatives and friends, calling them not only by their Christian names, but also by the name of the tribe they belonged to.

Corliss once talked about something he had experienced as Victor. One day he had taken his fishing boat far out into one of the wide coves when his motor suddenly failed. He was tossed about in the waves having no control. When he saw a boat he put on a Salvation army uniform which he had on board since he thought that no one would take any notice of a waving Indian in a boat. To his amazement the boat came closer and took his boat in tow. Uncle Victor had told the story in the presence of Mrs. Chotkin a long time ago, but she was sure that no one could have told Corliss about it. Another time he said to his mother, "When the 'old dame' and me used to visit you we always slept in this room." Saying this he pointed to a room which was now used for other purposes. This too was true.

Many such memories would surface in him unexpectedly. When he was nine his memories of his previous life began to disappear. When Stevenson interviewed Corliss at the age of 15, the boy claimed not to be able to remember anything from his past life. All too often the diligent investigator Stevenson has failed to meet children at an age when they still had direct access to memories of their past lives. Therefore in many cases he has had to rely on other people telling him things afterwards. Most of the children who remember past lives begin to talk about these when they are about two years old. But after the age of six the memories usually become less frequent, and by the age of nine are often completely gone.

We have not yet finished the story about the Indian boy Corliss. Mrs. jockey Chotkin had always combed her son's hair to the back. Corliss always combed it to the front just like his deceased great-uncle used to do. He also had a stutter like him, just as he had mentioned to his niece in his previous life. When he was ten years old he started having speech therapy. This seemed to have cured him because when Stevenson spoke with him he no longer stuttered. Victor had been a very religious man, which was why he had joined the Salvation army. Corliss also developed similar views on life, which became noticeable when he avidly started reading the Bible and later decided to look for a Bible school. Victor had been a keen fisherman. He used to say that he would be happy to spend all his life out at sea. He had also been very good at fixing boat engines and anything involving the use of his hands. He could not have inherited this from his father since he apparently had no such skills. Corliss was also left-handed just like Victor had been.

If we stop to look at these statements a little more closely, we could well come to the conclusion that we bring our talents, peculiarities and physical attributes with us from our past lives, rather than inheriting them all from our parents. Think about which characteristics you have obviously inherited from your parents genetically and which completely different ones you were born with. These could possibly be ones you had in a previous life and have now brought these talents and characteristics with you into your present life.

It is important to note that Stevenson always inspected extremely carefully the birthmarks that babies were born with. The mark on the base of Corliss' nose was from a small operation that Victor had undergone in hospital in 1938. This mark was still visible after the operation, during which they had removed the right tear duct. But the larger mark on the back was not typical of a usual birthmark. It was about 2.5 centimetres long, dark in colour, slightly raised and about 0.5 centimetres wide. Stevenson writes, [8] "Along the edges of the main scar I could see small round marks on both sides. Four of these were in a straight line along one side like needle wounds received during surgery." Corliss must have scratched the scar for it was often inflamed. Stevenson had the hospital send him a detailed account of Victor Vincent's operation. Corliss' scar on his back perfectly matched the one Victor had been left with after his surgical operation. This case presents us with clear evidence in favour of reincarnation.

The great research scientist Stevenson has even more proof on offer, which I will speak about in detail in this book. We will now turn our attention to a case, which one of his students and research partners investigated in India using Stevenson's methods.

I DROWNED IN A WELL WHEN I WAS A YOUNG GIRL

The girl Manju Sharma was born in 1969 in a small village called Pasaulie in the state of Uttar Pradesh. She was born to a poor Brahmin family. When she was about two years old she began to talk about being from Chaumula (a neighbouring village approximately 5-6 kilometres away). She mentioned the names of both her father and brother from her previous life and said that her father had a shop. She spoke in detail about the day she died. As a nine-year-old girl she had just come home from school and had gone to the well to wash a statue of God. She had lost her balance and had fallen into the well and drowned. She gave her parents clear descriptions of her previous home, but her parents did not pursue the matter, since they thought that their daughter was probably making it all up. Perhaps they vaguely suspected that she could be telling the truth, and that she might be homesick for her previous family and wanted to return to them.

A few months later a man rode into their village on a bicycle to do some business. Later on, as he was about to get back on his cycle, the little girl Manju came running up to him, held on to his bicycle and said, "You are my uncle!" He then answered, "I don't know you. Whose daughter are you?" To which Manju replied, "You don't know me, but I know you. You are my father's brother. My father's name is Ladali Saran." The man was baffled since this name was correct. He assumed she was one of his brother's children, but could not remember which one of them for the moment He asked her how she came to be in this village. To this the two-year-old explained that she had fallen into the well when she was washing her statue. Only now did Babu Ram (this was his name) realise that she must be talking about a past life, for he remembered that one of his brother's daughters really had drowned in the well.

When Manju begged him to take her home with him, he promised her that he would do this some other day. When he returned to Chaumula he told his brother's family all about this encounter in Pasauli.

The first person to go and investigate this case was the drowned girl's mother (her daughter's name had been Krishna). She was intent on finding out, whether this story really had something to do with her sadly missed child. When she returned to her family, she assured them that the girl really was her daughter reborn. Next Krishna's brother went off to find out for himself whether the girl's statements were true. He soon returned utterly convinced. By now even the father was keen to find out whether or not the girl really was his deceased daughter reborn. On meeting her he asked her many questions about the life of his deceased daughter, all of which the girl was able to answer correctly. Krishna's parents now begged Manju's parents to allow them to take their daughter on a visit to Chaumula. They agreed to this under one condition, that her brother could accompany them. When they arrived at her previous home Manju recognised many things, especially those that had belonged to her.

When the parapsychologist Dr. Pasricha visited the now eight year old Manju, she was told that Manju still visits her previous parents in their village from time to time. The research scientist was able to establish for certain that neither of the families had known of each other before these events occurred. This fact brought her to the conclusion that no information could have been transferred to Manju consciously or subconsciously. Dr. Pasricha was able to verify 19 out of 23 statements that Manju had made. The remaining four could not be proved. Manju married in 1988 but still remained in contact with her previous family. By that time she had forgotten most of the details from her past life apart from those relating to her tragic death.

I would like to point out something of interest. Manju had always refused to go to the well. Reincarnation therapy has made it clear to me that certain things, situations or people which had something to do with the cause of our death in a previous life, seem to create inexplicable aversions in our present lives. Our subconscious wants to protect us from getting into a similar potentially harmful situation again. Think about it for a moment, what do you have an aversion to? The more acute these are, the more devastating the event must have been that imprinted itself on your subconscious.

After Dr. Pasricha had meticulously researched many cases of reincarnation among children, she wanted to determine how many Indians were able to remember past lives at a young age. She trained a large team of helpers for this investigation. From 1978 to 1979 this team of helpers questioned 8611 people in nine villages in the province of

Agra. They asked them whether as a child they were able to remember past lives and whether they talked about this to anyone at the time.

Nineteen people claimed to have been able to recall past lives while they were children. Now came the task of asking their relatives and acquaintances whether they could remember this person as a child making comments about there past life. All 19 cases were verified. If we were to do some calculations we could arrive at the conclusion that one in 450 Indians remembers a past life and had talked about it to others during their childhood. The scientist Dr. Pasricha commented saying, "These numbers are only a rough guide. We must not generalise since this investigation only covered a small area."[9] Those of us who are involved in spreading the truth must be thankful for the work of such dedicated scientists as Stevenson, Pasricha, Banerjee, Haraldsson and many others. All of them use scientific means to get to the truth about reincarnation in order to establish whether such a thing as repeated lives on earth really exist.

Now let us look at another research scientist, originally a colleague of Stevenson, who later carried out his own research projects on the subject of reincarnation, and later gained a teaching qualification at the University of California. He is also the publisher of the *Journal of parapsychology*.

THE BOY WHO CRIED OUT FOR
HIS DAUGHTER IN HIS SLEEP

The Indian professor Dr. H. N. Banerjee, who apart from Professor Stevenson and Professor Haroldsson is probably the most well-known research scientist on the subject of reincarnation, became famous in the USA by bringing the case of Joe Wilke to the attention of the public.

A three-year-old girl from Iowa suddenly told her parents that she used to be called Joe Wilke. She was growing up in a strictly Catholic family in which any discussion on the subject of reincarnation was forbidden. The girl also told her parents that her wife was called Sheila and that they had both been fatally injured in a motorbike accident on the 20th July 1975 in Brookfield Illinois. Professor Banerjee had heard of the claims this girl had made and asked her to tell him everything once more. He then wrote to Dr. Adrian Finkelstein, who was living in Chicago, asking him to find out whether there was any truth in what the girl was saying. Dr. Adrian Finkelstein wrote back saying: The police investigation stated that a Joseph Wilke and his wife from Brookfield had died on the 20th July 1975 at 5:33pm in an accident involving his Honda motorbike.

A sceptic could well say that someone was playing games with Dr. Banerjee by telling a three-year-old girl about an accident he had heard about, and then telling the girl to recount the story to the research scientist as if it was her own from a past life. A little girl would not fool Professor Banerjee, an experienced research scientist. I will now tell you about another case that this Professor investigated, and which in my eyes is even stronger proof of reincarnation.

In Adana, on the southern coast of Turkey, lived Mehemet Altinklish and his family. One-day his two-year-old son said to him, "I don't want to live here any more. I want to go back to my home and children." His father said, "What did you just say Ismail?" "Don't call me Ismail, my name is Abeit," the child replied. His father then wanted to know from where he got these ideas. His son explained that his real name was Abeit Suzulmus and that he had been the owner of a large garden nursery until three men had broken in and killed him.

His father clearly remembered that several months before the birth of his son, a man named Abeit Suzulmus, the owner of a large garden centre who lived just over a kilometer away from Mr. Altinklish had been killed with an iron bar by three men. There had been many newspaper reports about this incident, which had happened on the 31st January 1956. Mr. Suzulmus had employed three men who applied for a job in one of his garden centres. These three men had locked him into a shed and had murdered him. After that they had broken into the house and had killed his second wife and her two children. The three murderers were caught. After a sensational trial two of them were hanged, while the third died in prison.

Ismail continued to insist that he is Abeit and repeatedly begged his father to take him to his previous home. He often cried out in his sleep, "Gulsarin! Gulsarin!" and woke up crying. His parents knew that this person he was calling in his sleep was his daughter from his past life, since he had told his parents about her. When Ismail was three years old his father finally agreed for him to be taken to the house of the murdered gardener.

Eleven people accompanied him. Ismail insisted that no one should show him where the house is, for he claimed he could find his way there. Even though his companions tried to mislead him several times Ismail continued on his way knowing exactly where he was going. The boy had never walked this way before.

When they had entered the house there were about 30 people waiting for them. They wanted to put the boy to the test to see whether he would recognise members of his former family. He immediately went up to one of the women, called her by name and told the others that this was his first wife. Then he saw his former daughter whom he had called out by name with such longing in his sleep. The same happened with his second daughter and his son who were also present. Finally he said, "Now I want to show you where I was murdered." He led them to the shed in which the brutal crime had been committed. There he pointed out certain things that had since changed.

All these events occurred in a Moslem country in which the Islamic Church forbids the belief in reincarnation and has certainly never taught it. There are smaller sects such as the Alevites and the Sufis, who do believe in reincarnation.

The newspapers published two articles about this family reunion. One story read as follows: The boy Ismail had recognised an ice cream vendor and had called him by name asking him, "Do you remember me?" The man said no, and Ismail continued, "I am Abeit. In the past you used to sell watermelons and vegetables instead of ice-cream." The salesman agreed that this was so. The boy also told him that he had been the one who had circumcised him long ago. By now the ice-cream salesman was also convinced that this boy had really been the nursery owner he had once known.

One day Ismail met a man and reminded him that he had lent him some money when he was Abeit, and that he still owed this money to the Suzulmus family. The man agreed that this was true. Another time he saw a man who was leading a cow on a rope. Ismail talked to him and asked whether that was the 'yellow one' that used to belong to Mr. Suzulmus. The man told him it was.

Professor Banerjee is absolutely convinced that none of these stories were invented. The two families had nothing to gain by telling lies, since that could well bring them into conflict with their religious leaders. When Professor Banerjee was investigating this case and was interviewing the families, he was asked to keep quiet about the things he was told. Besides those families avoided each other. The murder victim's family was probably accusing Ismail's family of having started all this talk.

As you can see from this story, children's memories of past lives are not restricted to countries in which the belief in reincarnation is common, but are also found in those where such a belief is frowned upon.[10] Let us now have a look at Sri Lanka, a country in which the belief in reincarnation forms an important part of the state religion. I am now going to introduce you to the famous Professor of Parapsychology and Reincarnation. His name is Professor Erlendur Haraldsson. In 1992 he was asked as Congress reporter to bear witness to my group regression, in front of an audience of approximately 400 people in Dusseldorf. The question addressed during this Congress was: *Is there life after death?*

THE GIRL WHO COMPLETED A DRAWING FROM HER PREVIOUS LIFE

When Dilukshi was two years old her parents became rather disturbed by the fact that she always called them aunt and uncle instead of mother and father. The child also repeatedly begged them to take her home to her real parents in Dambulla. Her parents scolded her for talking such nonsense, but the child was quick-witted saying, "My real parents never scolded me, instead they called me 'darling' and 'dear little daughter'." She also told her parents that she had drowned in the river near the village. Finally her parents went to seek advice from the monks in the nearby monastery. They were so fascinated by this case that they told Mr. Abeypala, the journalist. He then wrote an article for the *Weekend* magazine telling the girl's story.

A rice farmer from Dambulla read this report. It reminded him of his daughter Shiromi, who had drowned in a nearby river on 19th September 1983, which was one year before Dilukshi's birth. The farmer and his wife wrote to the newspaper telling them about the death of their daughter, and also of their willingness to be introduced to the girl. I can well imagine how pleased the journalist must have been, to be given the opportunity to research this case for his newspaper. As a journalist he was used to reporting on past events, whereas this case was yet to unfold.

The journalist arranged to meet Dilukshi and her parents, and together they drove about 100 kilometres, which brought them within walking distance of the village. From there they walked the last few kilometres along the paddy fields. The journalist's report went as follows: "This was a strange story — to be reborn and then to find her parents from a previous life once more. Things like this are extremely rare, even in Sri Lanka. I was fortunate enough to be witness to the girl recognising her parents from the past. She not only recognised them, but also her brother, her sister, her aunt and her grandmother. I was witness to all of this. I had seen enough not to need any further proof." They then fetched the toys and clothes that had belonged to the deceased girl, all of which Dilukshi recognised immediately. Apart from her clothes there was her drinking flask for school, her blackboard, her pencils her sunglasses and many other things. When she was given a book of her drawings from the past, she found one that she had not been able to finish at the time, so she immediately sat down and completed the picture.

When Dr. Haroldsson later heard about these events, he wanted to carry out further investigations using all the scientific means available to him. He claimed that this case was lacking in hard evidence. He thought the girl should have been presented with all sorts of things, instead of only her own. In this way she could then have been asked to point out the ones she recognised as her own from her past life. They had missed a good opportunity, but there was still enough material that could be used as evidence for this case. For instance, when the girl was taken down to the river, she pointed out the exact place where she had drowned. She picked up a stone and threw it in that direction full of contempt. Children often react like this in situations where they want to demonstrate their anger.

Some years later, when Professor Haraldsson took the English publisher Jeffrey Iverson to show him the river, he mentioned that before Dilukshi was taken there, she had mentioned seeing a suspension bridge directly above the place where she had drowned. By the time she was taken there the bridge had been demolished. Even so her claims had been correct. Before being taken to the river Dilukshi had also mentioned that the roof of her parents house could be seen when standing on a small rock. When Mr. Iverson stood on the rock, sure enough he could see the roof of the house. During a film that Mr. Iverson was making based on the theme of reincarnation, Dilukshi and her parents were asked for their co-operation. The girl felt completely at home with her previous family, and had brought her 'parents' a small present. Geoffrey Iverson realised that he had witnessed a family reunion that was both joyful and sad. The rice farmer's family must have rejoiced at the fact that their deceased daughter was once more alive, but may have been a little saddened by the fact that she now belonged to another family.

Professor Haraldsson informed the English journalist, that there are 17 proven facts regarding this case, 15 of which have yet to be proven for certain. Dilukshi had talked about a vegetable stall, which now no longer existed. She had also mentioned that the owner had been a very thin young man, but until now no one had been able to trace a man of this description. Haraldsson showed the film crew where the shop had once been, at which moment a thin young man happened to come out of his house. Professor Haraldsson asked the young man whether he used to sell vegetables here. The man told them that that was correct. When asked about

Shiromi, he said that he remembered her well, since she regularly used to come into his shop. When they asked him about the thin young man Dilukshi had talked about, he explained that he was that man and that he had always been called the 'thin brother'. [11]

My guess is that after hearing of such extensive evidence, the possibility of returning to earth again and again will have become far more feasible. For some reason, every case seems to have a few gaps in the evidence for which we are sometimes unable to find the missing links. Even so, I am convinced that if you read all the evidence available to you in this book, you will no longer be able to deny the existence of reincarnation.

A BOY DISCOVERS THE NAME OF HIS MURDERER FROM THE PAST

In December 1983 a boy named Titu Singh was born in a village near Agra. At the age of four he began to insist that his name was Suresh Verma, and that his wife Uma and his two children lived in Agra and were owners of a radio shop. He begged his present parents to take him back home and continued to reject them as his real parents. The entire family was tired with the intense behaviour of the boy, who insisted on being called Suresh and continually asked to go to Agra. He also talked about having been murdered by two men. He could clearly remember what had happened to him:

One day as he had arrived home in his car and had sounded his horn so that his wife would open the gate, two men came running towards him and had shot him in the head. He knew the names of the two men. The one that had fired the shot was a businessman called Sedick Johaadien.

During a stay in Agra, Titus's older brother went to find out whether there really was a radio shop with the name his younger brother had mentioned. To his amazement he actually found a radio shop with the name 'Suresh radio shop'. He went in and asked to see Suresh Verma. He was told that Suresh had been the owner of the shop but had died several years ago. When he asked for more information about the owner's cause of death, he was advised to go and visit the deceased man's widow Uma Verma.

Uma Verma told him that her husband had been shot in front of their house after returning home in his car. No one knew who had shot him and therefore the murder had been unsolved.

Titu's brother then informed Uma that his little brother claims to be her deceased husband. He told her everything that Titu had talked about at home. Suresh's widow now insisted on going to see the boy herself. She also told the rest of her family about this incident, so Suresh's parents and his three brothers all decided to join her.

When Titu saw his parents and his wife he was so happy he ran up to them and hugged them all. Then he drummed on a stool with his hands to vent his joy just like Suresh used to do when he was a child. A decision was made with his parent's permission to take Titu to Agra to confirm his past life memories.

Once they had arrived there his brothers wanted him to show them the way to the radio shop. They tried to mislead him on purpose, but the four-year-old was not fooled. Even when they told the driver to drive faster as they were approaching the shop, the boy suddenly shouted, "Stop! This is where my shop is!" After the boy had recognised several things from his past, his family was completely convinced that Titu really was their previously murdered son Suresh reborn. When Professor Chatdah from the University of Delhi heard of this incident he immediately showed great interest in the case. He visited Suresh's widow Uma and asked her what it was that had finally convinced her that this boy really was her deceased husband reborn. She said that when she described an incident that only she and her husband knew anything about, Titu was able to remember it clearly. It had been about Titu having given his wife a big bag of sweets when they were out on a picnic.

Professor Chatdah must have told his colleague Professor Stevenson about this case, for Stevenson sent his colleague Antonia Mills to Agra to continue the research with Professor Chatdah. They wanted to clear their doubts regarding the authenticity of this case. All their research confirmed that they were dealing with an authentic case of reincarnation. Naturally they also inspected Titu's head to see if he had any scars or birthmarks relating to the shot in the head that had killed him in his previous life. To their amazement they found a dent on the right side of his head which was precisely like the mark a bullet entering the skull would leave. On the other side of his head where the bullet had left the skull in his previous life, they found a star shaped scar. The wound would naturally have been bigger than the one on the other side of Suresh's head, since a bullet leaving the skull would have made a larger hole than the one entering it.

Dear readers, aren't you left speechless after reading about this case? Naturally this is no proof for the hardened critic who doubts everything that reincarnation may try to prove. By the way, I forgot to mention that Titu later remembered the name of his murderer, and when the Agra police questioned the man he confessed to the murder. [12]

I think I have given you enough examples of children's memories of past lives. I could tell you dozens more interesting cases that have served as evidence of reincarnation. I will come back to the subject of children's memories later in order to give you the final evidence. Please allow me to present you with some cases of adults' memories of past lives.

2

ADULTS' MEMORIES OF PAST LIVES

A DÉJÀ-VU EXPERIENCE IN SALISBURY CATHEDRAL

Have you ever had the experience of being somewhere and suddenly everything seems very familiar, giving you the feeling that you have been there before? Yet you know full well that you have never been there before in your life, and have not seen the place on film. Thousands of people have had this experience. Others meet someone and are certain that they already know that person from somewhere else. Others again experience a situation and are convinced that they have already experienced exactly the same thing before.

Scientists speak of these experiences as *deja vu* experiences. This expression stems from the French language meaning *already seen*. Explanations of all kinds have been put forward to explain this phenomenon of *reliving*. Maybe Cryptomnesia has a part to play in this; which means that something that we once knew and then forgot suddenly comes to mind again, triggered by a similar or identical person, place, situation or even a feeling. Such déjà vu experiences are often associated with telepathy; namely the tapping into the thoughts or the subconscious of another human being, alive or dead, and suddenly seeing their memories as your own, thus triggering a déjà vu experience. It could also be that something we have dreamt about, without being able to remember it afterwards, suddenly happens in reality and again triggers a so called déjà vu experience. Scientists only consider the possibility of past life memories as a last resort, if at all in most cases.

For instance, if someone went on holiday to a completely new destination, and on arrival notices that it all seems terribly familiar without ever having seen a film report about the place, it could well be that this person has been there before, long ago in another life. This is what happened to the conductor Bruno Walter when he went to Vienna for the first time. This is how he describes the experience in his autobiography:

The whole of the city centre seemed very familiar. He knew that when he got to a street corner and turned right or left he would find certain buildings that he could describe beforehand. He told his friend and teacher Gustav Mahler about this experience, for he knew Mahler was a great believer in reincarnation. He probably explained this experience as some kind of memory of a past life. This experience and his teacher's explanation of it may have encouraged him to become an avid seeker of the truth and to study Rudolph Steiner's Anthroposophy.

In my opinion this case may not have anything to do with past life memories. We humans have the propensity to be extremely inquisitive. On going to sleep shortly before we are due to travel to a new holiday destination, we may well enjoy leaving our physical bodies and taking a trip on the astral plane, to see the foreign country we are about to visit. This may be exactly what happened to Bruno Walter, and he could have visited Vienna, the town of music, several times in his sleep, thereby later creating the opportunity for a déjà vu experience.

If one day you should have such an experience, try to find out whether, for instance the hotel, which you feel certain to have been in before, looks identical in all its details to the way you remember it. See if you can remember whether the flowerbeds, the trees or the colour of the hotel are identical in your memory to that which you are experiencing as deja vu. Should everything be the same as you remember, then in most cases these will be memories of an astral journey. If on the other hand you should discover that several things look a little different, i.e. the flowerbeds weren't there or are in a different place, that the trees were smaller or were somewhere else, or that the colour of the building seems different, then you could be dealing with a *similarity effect*. You have seen a similar situation or similar place somewhere before. Failing this you could really be remembering a past life.

I now want to tell you about a case of déjà vu that occurred in Salisbury Cathedral in England.

Mr. Richards is a banker in London. He had always been interested in the architecture of the Christian Middle Ages. He had never really thought about where his interest for this kind of architecture came from. One day he wanted to take a trip to Stonehenge with his wife by car, but it started raining. They decided to visit the neighbouring town of Salisbury and explore the cathedral until the rain stopped.

When they arrived and had entered the cathedral, Mr. Richard had a strong feeling of having been there before. This feeling gradually became more intense as everything seemed very familiar to him. When he looked up at the ceiling the feeling disappeared, but as soon as he looked at the walls it was there again. All of a sudden he had a vision in which he saw himself as a labourer. He was wearing simple clothes and was carrying stones and heaving them up with ropes. He saw the cathedral in the process of being built, at which stage it had no roof on it. He could clearly observe his work mates. Then he saw himself in a house. He knew he was married and could see his wife and children, with whom he lived in Salisbury. In short, he was experiencing everything as if it were in the present. This experience lasted only a few minutes and then was gone. He met up with his wife again and tried to tell her what had happened. It was as if he had just seen a film in which he played the leading role. Yet somehow it was more than a film since he could experience everything, the lifting of the heavy stones and the love he had felt for his family.

This example demonstrates clearly that this must have been a memory of a past life, since Mr. Richard had relived a certain stage of the Cathedral's development. The images and impressions were definitely not of today. His deja vu experience was definitely from a past life. Had this experience been about the same building a hundred years ago, when the cathedral had looked more or less as it does today, then he may not have been so convinced that his memories were of a previous life. He would then have had to look very closely at what the people were wearing and other such details that were different from today.[13]

Déjà vu experiences usually happen spontaneously and are often linked to places, people, situations or objects. However, during meditation these experiences can also occur quite independently of outside stimuli, especially when one is in a relaxed frame of mind.

The following report is an extract from Yonassan Gershom's sensational book, **Do victims of the Holocaust return?** Many of my clients who come to me for regression therapy with symptoms such as asthma, nightmares or weight problems, often discover that these symptoms are after-effects of the trauma they experienced during the Holocaust. In his book Rabbi Yonassan Gershom focuses on reports from both Jewish and non-Jewish people relating to their previous life experiences of the Holocaust.

THE MAN WHO REDISCOVERED A CLOCK FROM HIS PAST LIFE

Mr. Whittier grew up in a Canadian village of 1600 inhabitants. There were no Jews in this village and before Mr. Whittier came across Rabbi Gershom he had never met any Jewish people, apart from two very fleeting encounters. He also had no Jewish ancestors. His upbringing was rather strict and his parents completely immersed him in their Christian beliefs. He later joined the Pentecostal Church where he learnt to speak in tongues in accordance with the Pentecostal teachings of the New Testament. The members of this sect are convinced that whoever is able to speak in tongues, usually in old languages such as Armenian or Hebrew, is touched by the Holy spirit who speaks through them. He was told that the language the Holy spirit was speaking through him was Jewish. He had never heard this language, nor did he know which country it originated from. Mr. Whittier also had an aversion to pork. When he was rummaging through some second-hand clothes in a shop one-day, he found two small round head coverings that he bought and now enjoys wearing at home. He only found out later on that these were Jewish *Kippas*.

In April 1991 he started having a recurring dream which continued to repeat itself for two weeks. The story unfolded in a series of episodes depicting a life in which he was a Jew during the Second World War in Holland. He saw himself in a cellar wherein he and his family were hiding from the police and the SS. They were hoping to avoid being taken away like so many other Jews, so they remained hidden in the cellar behind sacks of potatoes. They had brought very little with them from their flat. Among the things they had brought was a clock which was very valuable and which the family was rather attached to. Their dog was also seen as part of the family and was in hiding with them.

In his dream Mr. Whittier saw himself taking his black and white dog out into the garden just before dawn. The dog suddenly sensed danger, and a voice was heard coming from the darkness. The dog leapt at the intruders, an SS officer, who immediately shot it, and then arrested Mr. Whittier.

Mr. Whittier usually felt very disturbed on waking from these dreams. Towards the end of his third dream he was told that the clock was now in Canada and that he could find it in an antique shop in Bundesstr 1 in New Scotland. The memory of these dreams usually stayed with him after waking. Who had spoken to him in the dream? Could it have been the Holy Spirit who had often spoken through him in foreign tongues in the past?

He decided to follow up the clue about the clock at the very next opportunity. Meanwhile he was given even more advice in his dreams. He never imagined that this could have something to do with a past life, since his Church strictly forbade the belief in this *superstition*. In a following dream he saw soldiers on horseback leading him to an open mass grave along with other men and women, including his wife. They were all dressed in prison clothing. When they got there they were shot and thrown into the grave.

Once these dreams had stopped, Mr. Whittier and a friend decided to go and see if the antique shop really existed in Bundesstr. They found an antique shop that was particularly noticeable because of its old-fashioned writing on the sign. They went into the shop that had many valuable antiques on display. They looked around but could not find the clock. Feeling disappointed, they were just about to leave the shop when the owner came in through the back door and closed it behind him. They could now see a clock, which until then had been hidden from sight by the open door. Mr. Whittier stood spellbound in front of the clock, for he suddenly realised that this was the clock he had often seen in his dreams, and knew that it had once belonged to him. But how could this be possible, when according to his belief repeated lives on earth did not exist? Mr. Whittier asked the owner of the shop where all these lovely antiques had come from. The owner told him that he had recently returned from a business trip to Holland where he had purchased the goods at an auction. The authorities had finally released these confiscated goods most of which had belonged to the Jews. In this way the antique dealer had been able to acquire a large amount of new stock. When Mr. Whittier enquired whether the clock had also come from there, the dealer said it had. After having been told the price of the clock Mr. Whittier realised he could not afford it and so he and his friend left the shop.

Mr. Whittier could not forget this clock or his dreams. He even continued to have more dreams. Every time he sat down to relax and think about the events he had seen in his dreams, other memories of his past life in Holland began to surface.

He heard about a regression therapist who could put people into a trance, enabling them to remember their past lives. People claim to have relived there past lives in such a realistic way that they were no longer in any doubt about the truth of what they had experienced during regression. Mr. Whittier arranged to see this regression therapist.

During regression he was able to relive every detail surfacing from his subconscious about his past life as a Dutch Jew called Stefan Horwitz. He saw how he and other members of his family had hidden themselves in his grandfather's vegetable cellar. His wife had found a way of moving a sack of potatoes with a rope, which closed the entrance gap making it impossible for unwelcome visitors to see anything unusual in the cellar. He also saw the clock again, which had been a family heirloom. Then he relived the beating that the men from the SS had given him, to make him disclose their hiding place in the cellar. Everyone who was hiding in the cellar was taken away by lorry and later put onto trains. He witnessed every detail right up to his gruesome death, and everything his dreams and the sudden flashbacks had revealed to him was confirmed.

During regression he was also able to experience what happened to him immediately after he had been shot. He was floating in light and saw his wife Helen stretching her arms out towards him. In this after death experience the meaning of his earthly life was revealed to him. I recommend that you read a more detailed description of this in the relevant book.

Mr. Whittier later wrote to Rabbi Gershom saying, "After this incredible vision of life after death, I was finally able to free myself of the pain and fears associated with my memories of the Holocaust."

Rabbi Gershom often talked about this story which Mr. Whittier from Canada had shared with him. On hearing this story, a number of people got together and made a collection in order to buy the clock. On the 19th May 1996 Mr. Whittier once again became the proud owner of it.

From these reports you can see that dreams can often be very meaningful. Sometimes they will reveal information about past lives, which surface from the subconscious, the super conscious or some other source. Many people have their first past life experiences in their dreams, which are often only perceived as the truth when information from other sources points to the same thing.

I have taken the following case from Brad Steiger's book *You will live again*. I once visited Brad in the eighties in Scottsdale, Arizona, where he was living with his second wife, Francie. Brad is one of the most sought-after authors of factual literature on Parapsychology in the United States. He has written over 140 books, has appeared in countless TV programmes and works endlessly to spread the knowledge of eternal truth, which we seem to have lost in our technical world, in a way that can be easily understood by everyone.

REUNITED WITH A BROTHER FROM A PAST LIFE

Dr. Allen Haimes had a recurring dream that started when he was a young boy. In these dreams he saw himself in a desert wrapped in the clothes worn by desert dwellers. These dreams usually ended when he sank into what he thought was sand, while hearing a woman's voice calling, "Suliman!" Each time he woke up just before he died feeling disturbed and drenched in sweat. These dreams occurred frequently when he was a boy. He did not know what 'Suliman' meant. Was it a person, a place or something completely different? Apart from studying medicine he also studied Middle

Eastern archaeology and developed an almost obsessive interest in the pyramids. He had visited the Middle East, but for some reason had not fulfilled his wish of travelling to Egypt. For his 40th birthday his wife presented him with a trip to Egypt. Soon after they travelled there together.

During a boat trip up the Nile they stopped at a town called Edfu. As they strolled hand in hand through the narrow streets, both of them suddenly had the feeling that it was all very familiar to them. To Judith it seemed like she could even understand the language of the local people. When they strolled through the temple of Luxor, Allen noticed that the Egyptian tourist guide looked exactly like one of the people he had seen in his dreams. He confided in his wife his knowledge of having lived in Egypt over a 1000 years before, and that the tourist-guide had been his brother in a past life. His older brother's name had been Ahran in his dreams.

Then the following happened. When the tourist guide laid eyes on Allen he immediately paused in the middle of his speech and gazed into Dr. Haimes eyes as though hypnotised. Then everyone else also looked at the American, who had apparently made the tourist guide lose his train of thought. Allen felt a little disturbed by this and led his wife away from the group. They both caught a taxi back to the boat on the Nile. Allen could not stop talking about his past life in Egypt. In the evening they received a call from the boat reception telling them that they had a guest waiting to see them.

When they arrived at the reception a man got up from his seat and came over to meet them. It was the Egyptian tourist-guide whom they had met that afternoon. Judith saw Allen go white. The Egyptian held out his hand and introduced himself as Emil. He told them he had something important to discuss with them. He mentioned that he was a Christian, but that he believed in reincarnation. Disturbing dreams about his past lives had plagued him in his youth. Emil said, "Today, when I looked into Alan's eyes during the talk at the temple, I knew that we had once been related to each other. I know that we lived in Edfu about a 1000 years ago."

Emil now described many events from there past life together, while Allen noted it all down on the back of an envelope. Judith had also become a member of that family in those days by marrying Allen. They had both moved to Luxor after the wedding. Allen then asked him which profession he had followed in those days. Emil told him that Allen had become a writer Dr. Allen Haimes. Emil being the oldest of the family would traditionally have taken up this profession, and followed in the steps of his father, but his right-hand was crippled and not suited to writing.

It had also been Allen's job in those days to count the sacks of wheat when they were delivered. He had to sort them out and arrange for their transport to the grain silos. It was there that he had fallen into the wheat and had drowned in it. Allen had been under the impression that he had died in quicksand, but it had never really made sense to him. Now he finally knew the truth of the matter. Emil continued his story saying that he and Allen's wife had accompanied him to the wheat silos. When he had fallen into the wheat his wife had let out a terrible scream and had called out his name, "Suliman!" When Allen heard this he had to sit down. He had finally found out who it was that had called Suliman in his dreams. It had been his wife from his past life, whom he had once again married in his present life. Judith and Allen became good friends with Emil and visited him several times in the following years. [15]

Do you find yourself being particularly interested in a certain time in history, or a particular historical event, or even in a certain famous person from the past? Perhaps this interest is so pronounced that you buy yourself books relating to that historical event or person? Sometimes such an interest can become a real passion or even an obsession. I know people who read or watch relevant films about everything to do with Alexander the Great for instance, or about the Roman Emperors or Napoleon, Metternich, or Bismarck, about the 30-year-war, the seven-year-war or the Second World War. There are collectors who only collect things from a certain time in history for instance, articles about the Biedermeier era, or of the time of the great founders or art nouveau. As far as I know from my work as a regression therapist, these people really did live in those particular times relating to their present day interests. We tend to be drawn to things that were dear to us or to those that caused us a lot of pain in the past. The next story was taken from a book by Dr. Frederick Lenz, and is about an American businessman who became passionately interested in the American Civil War of the last century.

MEMORIES AWAKENED ON THE BATTLEFIELD

Alexis is a retired businessman from South Carolina. He has always been fascinated by the American Civil War for as long as he can remember. This war was fought in the United States between 1861and 1864. The soldiers from the northern states set out to fight the soldiers from the southern states. This war was mainly about freeing the black slaves in the southern states. Even as a young boy Alexis had always wanted to play the role of a Confederation army soldier. His passion for the American Civil war became an obsession. He read many books on the subject and joined a fan club for people like him who have a fascination for this war.

There are several of these fan clubs in America, which almost exclusively focus on this particular war, be they in the northern or southern states. Some of the members even dress in the respective uniforms. Many of them, especially those who are part of a strict Church religion, do not believe in past lives even though you could bet that most of them had somehow been heavily involved in that war in a previous incarnation. If any of them were to visit a regression therapist to discover whether or not they were alive at that time, they would almost certainly discover that this had been so. My regression seminars have given hundreds of people the chance to relive certain historical events which they have been actively or passively involved with for years.

The part of this civil war that Alexis was most captivated by was the battle of Gettysburg, which took place in 1863 and ended with the victory of the northern states. He even gave talks about this battle at his club. One day when he was preparing for another talk, he once again visited the huge battlefield. It has since become a historical monument and is visited by thousands of people on pilgrimages every year. When walking across these huge fields he was suddenly transported to a completely different time where he found himself in the midst of a battle as a soldier of the Confederation. There was a strong smell of gunpowder in the air. The sound of canons was like thunder. He could hear the screaming of the wounded and officers shouting orders. Then he saw the closed ranks of the Union soldiers marching towards him and his comrades. Suddenly he felt a sharp pain in his leg and knew he had been shot. One of his comrades bent down to expose the wound and bandage it up as best as he could. Then four soldiers in blue uniform appeared and shot them both. His comrade was fatally wounded and fell down on top of him. He was then shot in the stomach, felt a sudden burning pain and found himself back in the present again.[16]

People who died from a fatal wound in a past life often have either a scar in exactly that area, or an inner weakness in that part of their body. Some may suffer from frequent chronic pains in the stomach, even after thorough examinations doctors can find nothing medically wrong. It is often concluded that the person is either imagining the sickness or is a hypochondriac. In the following part of the book I will explain in more detail how regression therapy can help people with such pains. When someone has experienced a horrific death at the hands of a person or in a particular situation, it is common for him to develop a fear of anything related to that past experience. The more gruesome and drawn out the death was, the more intense will be the *after effects* in his present life. Maybe Alexis' death as a soldier on the battlefields of Gettysburg was very quick, for even today he still has a great admiration for the life of a soldier in the civil war.

Let us look at some past memories that deal with love at first sight, and relate to a lover from a past life.

REUNITED WITH A LOVER FROM A PAST LIFE

A production assistant told Brad Steiger the following story. One day she went to a stud farm to take one of the horses out for a ride and in the stalls she met a young man. When they looked at each other she felt a strange closeness to him. She found herself greeting him with the name Wesley, which just came into her mind. The boy replied using the name Lillian. Neither of them felt that they had invented those names. They immediately felt completely at ease with each other, and continued to have a platonic relationship. The only explanation they could find to explain their unusual attraction to one-another was the possibility of having known each other in a past life. They continued to call each other by these names from the past life.

One night the woman had a terrible dream that was too powerful to dismiss as *just a dream*. She was a young woman living in a small town in South Dakota in the middle of the 18th century. She saw fruit trees and unpaved roads winding their way through the small town. Her husband from that time stood in front of her, he was extremely angry. He had found out about an affair she had had with a young man. Her husband had thrown oil lamp at her in his anger. The oil leaking out set fire to her clothes, and she was burnt to death. Then she saw herself outside of her body. She could see her young lover Wesley approaching the house. The flames had already engulfed the entire room and he was unable to reach her. He guessed what had happened, and fetched his gun and shot his lover's husband in the stomach. Lillian was able to watch from above how Wesley was hung for this murder.

One could of course dismiss this case as just a nice story; by arguing that as an excuse for her attraction to a handsome young man she had searched for explanations in her dreams, and her subconscious had then spun her this yarn. Yet the strange thing was that on the very same morning the young stable boy awoke from a terrible nightmare. His parents had heard him call the name 'Lillian' in his sleep. In his dream he was trying to rescue her from the fire. He later told his friend Lillian that his dream had taken place in a small town and that she had been his sweetheart at that time. They had kept their meetings very secret, since she was married. They told each other everything they had dreamt and realised that all their dream experiences coincided with one another's.[17]

Let us now examine another case in which two people experience love at first sight, and only later discover that there past life experiences played a part in their present relationship.

LOVE IN THE PRESENT, BALANCES UNFULLFILLED LOVE FROM A PAST LIFE

John and Alison met at a party in 1967. He was a law student and she was a representative for a telephone company. They immediately felt attracted to each other, and it wasn't long before they told each other how they felt. The following year they were married and moved into the student quarters at Cambridge. They both felt that they had known each other for a long time. A few years later John had a vision in which it was revealed to him where they had originally known each other. It happened one evening when they were sitting in bed looking at each other. In John's eyes Alison's face suddenly changed appearance completely, as did the whole room. This vision was superimposed on top of his present reality. He saw himself and his wife wrapped in old-fashioned clothes, and the walls were clad in carpets. He knew that they were in England in the Middle Ages. They were both in love with each other, but the girl's parents had already arranged a marriage for her. She was so distraught about not being able to marry the man she was in love with that she poisoned herself. When he heard about this he was utterly devastated and decided to leave England for good. He signed up with the army and threw himself headlong into various battles in order to meet his own death. He finally returned to England and spent the rest of his years as a monk in a monastery. This vision only lasted a few minutes and yet it seemed as though he had seen an entire film. It became very clear to him that this was the reason for their present relationship. In this life they needed to complete what they were unable to finish in the past. [18]

I think they may both have had some lessons that remained from their past, or there was still a karmic debt to pay. As a regression therapist I have frequently observed that the spiritual and physical suffering of my clients stems from a past life in which they were the cause of someone else's pain and suffering. So it could be that in a former life Alison was the one who denied her daughter the freedom to marry the man she loved, thereby causing her to take her own life. John could well have been the daughter's father. As human beings we only seem to understand God's laws by experiencing precisely that which we inflict on others. This law of karmic debts serves our spiritual development. It is always just and has nothing to do with punishment. Its sole function is to help us realise and understand things through experience. Whatever situation that we have to deal with in our present life can often be traced back to karmic debts. Karma can also work itself out in a positive way. If for instance someone did something very good in the sense of God's laws, he can then reap the rewards in his present life. Whatever we do to another in thought, word or deed will return to us in equal measures. If you want to have a blessed, peaceful future life, then you must see to it that you are loving to others in thought, word and deed in this life.

REUNITED WITH HER CHILDREN FROM A PAST LIFE

Jenny Cockell was born in England in 1953. There was usually a lot of tension in her house because her parents were not getting on very well. This may well be why Jenny was a introvert child who found it difficult to communicate with others about what was going on at home. Nevertheless she had clear memories of four of her past lives, from which she was constantly reliving various scenes. Most of her past memories consisted of a mother with eight children who devoted all her time caring for them. She knew she was called Mary and that she herself had been that mother. She saw herself walking through the village and going to the market. She saw her simple house from the outside and frequently from inside too. It was less than 1 km from the village centre and was surrounded by fields and trees. There was also a stream near by. On the other side of the road were the moors. She knew from the beginning that this country she remembered was Ireland. Her husband at the time often worked outside the house, while she dedicated herself completely to raising her children. She saw herself sewing, cooking and tidying up. She could see each of her children, clearly expressing their individual characters and ways of being. She found it hard to remember their names or even the name of the village.

There were several scenes from that life that were crystal clear. In one of these she saw herself wrapped in a long shawl standing by a wooden style. It was dusk, and she was waiting for a boat to come in.

At other times she saw the following: her boys had set a trap and had found a rabbit in it the following morning. They were pleased to have caught something, but she was unhappy about them having set the trap. Thankfully she could see the rabbit was still alive and was being set free.

When Jenny was four years old she confided something from her past lives to her mother. To Jenny the events from the past were real and she believed that she had really lived them. Her mother did not belittle her for telling her these things. She carefully listened to her, but as a strict Catholic she put these things down to wishful thinking rather than the truth. Jenny was very disappointed with her mother's attitude, and from then on she kept all her memories of her past lives to herself. Nevertheless she held to what she knew to be the truth. She even saw scenes from her past lives in her dreams.

One of these dreams was a terrible nightmare, which she had quite frequently. It was the experience of Mary's death at the age of 35 years. She saw herself in a hospital room with a high ceiling. She was aware of having a fever and was struggling to breathe. What she missed most was the contact with her children, which she was not permitted. Only her husband was allowed to visit her. Somehow she was aware of her imminent death. She had no fear of death but felt very angry, because letting go into the inevitable involved withdrawing from her children. They were her only concern. Then she saw herself outside of her body looking at her husband from above, who was sitting by her bedside. At that point she regularly woke up from her nightmare, still feeling angry at fate for leaving those children motherless.

Most of her past memories occurred during the day. When

she was older she drew some of the scenes from her memories, including the little house in which she had lived as Mary. She made maps of the village and all the roads and footpaths she could remember. She knew that the village was not far from her house and was situated north east of Dublin. One day she opened her school atlas and looked at maps of Ireland. She found a village called Malahide situated north east of Dublin. The roads leading to it coincided exactly with the ones she had drawn on her map. At the age of 27 she managed to buy a local map of Malahide. Comparing this map to the one she had drawn years ago and was surprised to find that she had put all of the main roads and important buildings in the right places.

At the age of 25 she subjected herself to her first regression under hypnosis. Her memories of her past lives were still clear at this time, especially her life as Mary. Her nightmare about her death had not surfaced for years. During regression she relived every detail from her past life, including her own death. She knew that she had had a still birth in one of the last years of that life, and that the doctors had warned her of the risks involved if she were to become pregnant again. She did not heed this warning and was soon expecting again. She died in 1932 after giving birth to a healthy girl whom she had named Elizabeth. She also remembered several of her children's names during regression; her oldest daughter having been called Mary after her.

Jenny was married by now with two children of her own. Her husband was very understanding about her need to find out more about her past life as Mary. In 1989 she travelled to Ireland to visit Malahide. When she arrived there she was shocked to see how much had changed in the last 56 years. New buildings and flats had sprung up everywhere. Where she remembered seeing a courtyard with two gates leading into it, there was now a supermarket. She found it difficult to imagine what it used to look like based on her memories of the past. Finally she found the path that led to her old house, but when she got there she only found an old ruin, and the nearby stream had become a mere trickle in a ditch. It was only after a second visit to Malahide that she was certain that this ruin really was the house from her past life. While walking about in it, memories and feelings came flooding back to her.

After having talked to people in the neighbourhood, she discovered that a John Sutton, his wife Mary and their children had once lived in that house. She then wrote several letters to various authorities hoping to find some documents about the Sutton family. She also tried to find them in the registers of christenings and deaths, and wrote to all the Sutton's she could find in the telephone book. She put advertisements in the local paper to find people who could give her more information about the Sutton family. She managed to find out that she was born in 1897 and died during childbirth in 1932, which she already knew from her own memories and through regression therapy. She found

six of her children's names and birth dates in the register
of christenings. Jefftrey Sutton had been born in 1923,
followed by his siblings Philomena, Christopher, Francis,
Bridget and finally Elizabeth. However these were only six
of her children and she was sure she had had eight. Only
later did she find out that she really did have eight children,
for the two that were not registered in that particular
register of christenings had in fact been christened in
another church. Their names were Sonny and Mary. She had
the good fortune of getting hold of the address of her oldest
son Sonny who was living in England at that time.

In 1990 Jenny was introduced to a journalist working for
television. He was very interested in her efforts to find her
past family. Jenny did not agree with all this becoming public
news at this early stage, but she was aware of the benefits
she could reap by co-operating with them, so she agreed.
Before introducing Jenny to Sonny, the journalist wanted
to film an interview with him, asking him questions about
his life in general, his youth in Ireland and especially about
life at home as a child. They thought it best that the 71-
year old was not told the true reason for this interview. Jenny
had specifically asked the journalists not to mention that
she was his mother, so as not to put him off. Even so Jenny
phoned Sonny Sutton just before the interview. She told
him about the dreams she has been having in which a woman
named Mary Sutton tells her about her life in Ireland giving
her detailed pictures. She went on to describe the house in
which Mary had spent her childhood from both outside and

inside. Mr. Sutton confirmed that all her statements were true. A date for their meeting was then arranged for the 23rd September 1990 at his house.

Jenny's husband and her two children accompanied her to Leeds, as they were keen to find out whether Jenny had really been Sonny's mother in the past. If both their statements were the same, they would have definite proof that Jenny had not been fantasising, and her memories of a life in Ireland as a child were the truth. Her reincarnation experiences would then be proven beyond any doubt. Even though Sonny Sutton was an elderly man by now, Jenny immediately recognised him by his mannerisms. She told him about her life in Ireland, and Mr. Sutton was amazed and had to agree that everything she said was the truth. The journalist who interviewed Mr. Sutton had asked him to draw an exact plan of the house in Malahide, from both inside and out. When Jenny showed him her sketches, which she had made many years ago when she was a young girl, he compared them with his own. To their amazement they were extremely alike. She kept saying to him, "Look at that, it's exactly the same as mine!" She then described the property and the neighbouring houses in detail. Sonny was amazed at the accuracy of her knowledge about his childhood.

Finally they talked about individual members of their family, and Jenny was able to describe them correctly, even down to their individual character traits. Then she described his mother and told him exactly what clothes she used to wear. Sonny even verified Jenny's claim that she wore her hair in a bun. Then the conversation focused on Mary's father who had been a stationmaster in charge of a level crossing. Apparently there was a signal box next to the crossing in which he often spent the night. Strangely enough Jenny could not remember much about her husband from that life. She was happy to be able to discover more about him from Sonny. She did remember him building roofs, and later going off to be a soldier in the First World War. The relationship between him and his wife could not have been very good, since John Sutton spent very little time at home. His son, who said that his father became an alcoholic and often gave him severe beatings, confirmed this.

Jenny told him about the trap his mother had talked about in which the children had caught a rabbit. This incident was deeply etched in his memory and he was able to fill her in on the details. He couldn't understand how this woman sitting opposite him, who was a total stranger, could know all these things. Jenny then asked him what his mother could have meant when giving her images of a woman standing on a wooden style at dusk waiting for a boat to come in. Mr. Sutton explained to her that she had been waiting for him, for every evening he used to row back from a neighbouring island in his boat. He was earning money there as a caddie. He earned two shillings and sixpence every day. He used to give his mother the two shillings and keep the sixpence for himself. Sonny could even remember the shawl his mother wore around her shoulders at the time. Sonny also confirmed that his mother had a still birth and had died in hospital in Dublin after giving birth to her youngest daughter. Her sons went to an orphanage and her daughters to schools belonging to the monastery.

Jenny had absolutely no doubt that this really was her oldest son from her past life in which she had been Mary Sutton. Then she told Sonny that it she herself who had been his mother. It took him some time to absorb this information. He finally accepted her for who she claimed to be and they formed a lasting bond between them.

With Sonny's help and her own investigations she was able to trace five of her seven children who were still alive. In 1993 there was a big family reunion with all of Mary Sutton's (now Jenny Cockell) five children. For the three brothers, not counting their brother Jeffrey who had died in 1985, this was their first meeting in a very long time. These brothers considered their sisters Phyllis (Philomena) and Betty (Elizabeth) lost or dead, since they had not been in contact with them for over 60 years. Their mother from a past life, who looked more like one of their daughters in age, had brought them all together again (apart from the two sisters who could not be traced). The television film crew was there to document this extraordinary reunion, so that it could be shown to their viewers. Sonny had asked his sisters what they thought about Jenny being their mother from a past life. They said that they could not accept reincarnation as a fact, since their Catholic Church did not teach this. Instead they chose to believe that their mother was working through Jenny from above in order to bring all the family members who were still alive together again.

Jenny was also able to remember a life between the one in Ireland and her present life in England. She was born as a boy in England in 1940, but died at the age of five from a viral infection. Her book, *Yesterday's Children*,[19] in which she describes her search for her children from a past life, became a best-seller and was translated into many languages.

Dear readers, what do you make of this successful search for children from another lifetime? Is this account not convincing evidence that reincarnation exists? It even gives strict religious believers something to think about. The conflict with the Church exists because the Church in the first 500 years after Christ taught the people about reincarnation, the earliest famous Church preacher having been Origines. Even Jesus acknowledged reincarnation by recognising John the Baptist as the reincarnation of Elias.

Even though regression plays a large part in the following two cases, I have included them in this section about adults' past memories because the actual memories already existed before regression took place. Delving deeper into their past lives, by using regression and hypnosis, the actual facts could be verified and checked against the person's spontaneous memories. In the following account a medium's claims are verified.

THE CHANNELLED PAST LIFE INFORMATION RECEIVED THROUGH A MEDIUM IS CONFIRMED

Dick Sutphen could well be called *Mr. Reincarnation of America*, for he is America's most famous promoter of reincarnation. Dick has written 14 books on the subject, has sold over 300 different tapes, videos, CDs and DVDs, has appeared in over 300 television programmes, and over 100,000 people have attended his group regression seminars. Apart from this he has been a pioneer in his research into regression therapy, and I feel fortunate to have been trained as a regression therapist by him. In his book, *You were born again to be together*,[20] he writes about a very interesting case.

Early in the Seventies he was leading a seminar at a centre for hypnosis, and the subject to be discussed at this seminar was *Group regressions into past lives*. One of his most successful students was Trenna, who after only a short time was able to put herself into a trance to relive her past lives. Dick and Trenna fell in love and moved in together. One evening while Dick was working at his desk, Trenna put herself into a trance in order to find out whether she and Dick had known each other intimately in a previous life. This is what she saw on her inner screen. She saw herself as a young Indian girl who at sunset was gazing across a grass covered hilly landscape and was waiting for some kind of decision or judgement to be made. Behind her in a teepee, she felt her tribe that was discussing this issue was against her. Then a tall Indian wearing a necklace came towards her, took her by the hand and led her into the circle of people. Then he gently patted her belly with his hand to indicate to the others that everything was well. Now the Indian girl knew that she was permitted to bear the child growing in her womb and would be allowed to keep it. She was overjoyed.

When Trenna had returned from this self-regression she went straight to her friend Dick and told him about what she had just experienced about him and her as Indians. Dick thought he wasn't hearing right because someone else had described the same events to him some time ago, in which he was also an Indian. Who had talked about this and where? He remembered visiting a well-known medium two years previously, whose name was Kingdon Brown. He could only vaguely remember what he had channelled, but he was certain that it was very similar to Trenna's story. He had never talked to her about it before. He remembered recording what Kingdon said at the time. He must have kept this tape somewhere. Dick suggested leading her into regression to find out more details about the life she had just glimpsed. Trenna agreed and saw herself as the Indian girl sitting in front of the tall Indian. He was disappointed in her. Dick carried on a conversation with Trenna, now as the Indian girl during this regression, asking her why the Indian was disappointed. She told him that she had been captured and taken away by a neighbouring rival tribe when the men of her tribe were out. She had been raped. She had managed to escape from the tribe and had found her way back to her people. The Indian who was now sitting opposite her had been her fiancée. He was disappointed in her for not having taken her own life after being raped. Everyone had looked at her with contempt on her return. Only this Indian now seemed to have changed his mind. Her fate was in his hands and depended on whether he would still take her as his wife, and whether he would allow the child to live.

As Dick allowed her to relive more of her previous life, she saw her growing son was considered to be an *outsider* with a dark past. When Dick encouraged her to move on to an event that was particularly meaningful to her, she saw her son being rewarded by his people for his bravery. He had been able to warn his tribe of approaching enemies and so had given them time to defend themselves. Shortly before her death, when looking back over her life, she told us that her son now had children of his own and that the most wonderful occasion in her life was when her son was finally accepted by his tribe.

The following day Dick searched among all his tapes and finally found the one with the medium's statements on it. During meditation, Kingdon Brown had described an Indian girl who was pregnant. Next he saw her carrying a child on her shoulders. Then the scene changed and he saw a tall Indian wrapped in a blanket, pacing up and down at sunset wrestling with the decision he had to make.

Then Kingdon had been silent for a while before saying, "He must decide whether a child that is soon to be born may live or must die." He turned to Dick and told him that he himself had been this Indian and that he had decided to let the child live.

In the past I spent much of my time visiting various mediums in foreign countries to find out more about myself and my past lives. This is something I have not pursued for some time now. What these mediums told me was often incorrect, vague, too generalised or simply wrong. Occasionally they are surprisingly accurate, as is the case in this example. In my opinion it is best not to depend on what they say, but rather to trust your own decisions. Even if it is the wrong choice we make, at least we can learn from it, and should the situation arise once more we will be all the wiser to make better choices. People who become dependent on the channelling of the medium are afraid of having to make their own decisions. But this is precisely what life is about, becoming responsible for our own actions. If we do find a reliable medium in order to receive guidance from the higher source to assist us in our spiritual growth, it can sometimes be of great help.

REUNITED WITH HIS WIFE FROM A PAST LIFE

Brad Steiger was told the following story: [21]

Roy and his son were rowing their boat across the Baker Lake in the northern states of Washington. Roy had recently joined one of the new Christian sects where he was baptised again. While out on the lake the feeling suddenly overwhelmed him that the lake, the mountains and in fact the entire landscape was familiar to him. He knew that he had seen all this before, but not on a map or in a film. Suddenly he saw himself alone in a canoe paddling across this lake. He had a different body and looked completely different, and was wearing the clothes of a trapper. This was a typical déjà-vu experience he was having. He was so completely convinced of the reality of this experience that he had to admit to these being memories of a past life.

This presented him with a huge conflict, whether to believe in reincarnation as a fact or believe that the devil had just played a trick on him. According to the beliefs of his sect there are of course no past lives, instead there is the devil who tempts us in devious ways in order to distract us from our beliefs, in order to take us into his domain which is hell itself. He continued to have flashbacks of a former life in which he was a trapper. Taking on board the beliefs of his religious sect, which to him was the only basis for happiness, he ardently prayed to God asking him to free him of those distracting images of a previous life. One-day when he was praying he heard what he thought to be God's voice. It told him that he would soon be meeting his wife from that life, whom he had loved very much.

This devil left him no peace. He secretly acquired books on reincarnation and finally plucked up courage to go and see a regression therapist to find out whether he really did live that life as a trapper in the north western states of America. In this regression he discovered the following that surfaced from his subconscious.

He was born just before the French Revolution and was called Jacques. His parents had fled to Canada with him. When he grew up he became a trapper who made a living from selling furs. His hunting grounds were the hills and woods in south west Canada and the north western states. Once he had succeeded in saving the chief of a tribe from an invading enemy, which gained him his friendship. This chief then offered him his stepdaughter in marriage and told him that she was the daughter of a white man. This man had been an alcoholic and had abandoned his daughter leaving her behind with the chief. The daughter was very frightened of her father because he had frequently mistreated her. The chief suspected that her father would soon return to fetch his daughter, Isabel, so he asked Jacques to take her into the forest with him. This he did in order to protect her from her father.

They set up camp by Lake Baker for the first few months. He fell in love with this girl and swore that he would never leave her. Later they moved to the coast at Puget Fjords where they built themselves a log cabin. They were very happy, apart from losing their son when she had a miscarriage. Sadly a bear killed Jacques before he was 30 years old.

During regression he was shown that Isabel had died shortly after him having lost the will to live and being extremely lonely.

Roy was now convinced of the truth regarding reincarnation for what he had seen in spontaneous flashbacks completely coincided with what he experienced during hypnosis. Even so this was not the end of the story.

Meanwhile he had divorced his first wife and even though he was now convinced of reincarnation he still remained part of his sect. In his Church he noticed a young woman and could not take his eyes of her. He immediately felt drawn to her, but his shyness would not allow him to speak to her. They continued to meet at church, until one day they spoke to each other and discovered that they both loved playing Bridge. From then on they met more often in a Bridge school. After such an evening when they were sitting in the car, Roy confided his secret to Susie. He told her that in a past life he had been a trapper in the north eastern part of the States, which is now the United States, and that he had lived there with a young woman in a log cabin... Here Suzy interrupted him saying that she knew that house. She then described the house in detail. Roy could not believe his ears. To his even greater amazement she added, "We had a still birth. It was a boy." Then Roy looked deep into her eyes. He was now convinced that he was really looking at the reincarnation of Isabel.

What was it the voice of God had said to him? Had he not spoken about introducing him to a woman whose name used to be Isabel? When he asked her how she knew that she had been that women, she told him that two years ago she had found out about this past life during a meditation and had written everything down. Then they hugged each other and cried tears of joy. She promised to show him her notes at their next meeting.

When Roy finally read Susie's notes he discovered that during her meditation a man named Jacques had come to her and had put his arms around her. He told her that they had both lived on the Puget Fjords at the end of the eighteenth-century. He had been a French trapper from Canada and that he would soon come to her because they belong together. He said that first he had a few things to deal with. He told her he had been born in France and that his parents had immigrated to Canada. Jacques also described the log cabin in which they had lived and the surrounding area. He also told her about the still birth of their son.

Susie had mentioned about this experience she had during meditation to a few close friends, who suggested that it might have something to do with the imminent meeting of her soul mate. After a year had passed she had put the notes away and no longer gave them any thought. Two weeks later she decided to drive 150 kilometres to Lake Baker where Roy had had his first déjà vu experience. When they got there Roy decided to walk in the woods to 'check the traps'. Suzie agreed and stayed near the lake where she wanted to meditate. As soon as Roy was out of sight Suzie began to panic, which was most unusual for her. She felt like screaming so that he would come back to her as quickly as possible.

When Roy returned from the woods, she told him about her fear that something might happen to him. Roy had since learned some regression techniques and suggested allowing him to lead her into regression that evening.

Susie then saw herself in a life as the daughter of a couple living in the eastern part of the United States. Her name was Isabel. Her mother died when she was very young. Her father turned to alcohol and often beat her or abused her sexually. When she was nine years old they had moved to the most western tip of this continent. There they had travelled on foot through the forest with a group of other men. It was here that her father had met the chief. She did not know whether this chief had bought her or had stolen her from her father. The chief treated her like a daughter. When she was about 12 years old rumours spread about her father returning to fetch her. This is why the chief had asked his white friend Jacques to take her into the forest until the danger was over. Jacques and Isabel had lived together by the lake. Her father had never found her. Sometime later they had moved to Puget Fjords, and lived there until a bear killed Jack. After that she had been too afraid to leave the cabin and had starved to death.

In this way they both saw their past lives from various angles. To her it was clear that all this was true about having lived in the woods. It was not long before they were a couple. I am tempted to write; And they lived happily ever after! The truth is often more real than anything our imagination can come up with. Many people have had the strangest outer and inner experiences, but are too afraid to tell anyone about them out of fear of not being understood or seen as insane. Maybe these people are not insane at all. Maybe we are just shortsighted or ignorant. There are so many things we do not understand, but given time our understanding will grow, if not in this lifetime then definitely in our future lives. Fifty or even twenty years ago the belief in reincarnation was limited to very few people in the West. Now this belief is spreading like wild fire, for the proven facts acquired through regression into past lives are overwhelming evidence. By having experienced thousands of regressions with individuals and in groups, I have become somewhat of an expert on the subject of reincarnation. I look forward to sharing some more of these experiences with you in the third part of my book.

3

THE EVIDENCE OF REINCARNATION REVEALED THROUGH REGRESSION THERAPY

THE DENTIST WHO HAD COLD SHIVERS RUN DOWN HIS SPINE

I have frequently mentioned the use of hypnosis in previous chapters. People often choose this method if they have had a déjà vu experience, or a dream about a past life. They usually want to discover whether what they saw was true, or to find out more about the events of that life. During hypnosis we get in touch with our subconscious, where everything we have ever experienced is stored, even those events that occurred thousands of years ago. All this is stored in our super memory bank (similar to that of a computer) which is situated in the right side of the brain.

As my first example in this section of the book I wish to

recount an experience which a dentist by the name of Dr. Bruce Goldberg had at the beginning of his career as a regression therapist. In October 1996 I went to visit Bruce at his home north of Los Angeles. We exchanged our experiences relating to regression therapy. He has since become one of the most sought-after authors and television guests dealing with the subject of reincarnation and regression. He could well be the most frequently engaged research scientist at present on the subject of trance induced regression. We talked with each other for over three hours. He put forward his ideas on how to break the cycle of reincarnation in our present lives. I mentioned the name 'Thayer', which will play a large part in the following story. Having studied the history of the middle ages and the old German language, I told him that this name could not have existed in Bavaria in the year 1200. Could this name perhaps have been spelt 'Theuer' or 'Deuer'? Bruce pronounced the name exactly the way he remembered hearing it from his client. The American pronunciation of European names and the way they spell them is often very different to the original name. This is why I shall use the spelling 'Theuer' for the young apprentice I am about to describe.

At the beginning of the 70's a man of around 40 came into Dr. Bruce Goldberg's hypnosis practice in Baltimore. The latter was a dentist and had learnt hypnosis in order to treat some of his patients without anaesthetic and still be totally pain free. He had read about trance induced regression and was now experimenting most successfully with this himself.

He soon became well known through his appearances on television in which he demonstrated his regression techniques. In his book *Past lives - Future lives* [22] he tells the story of a man who he calls Arnold in order to protect his identity. Arnold was a business agent for an appliance company. His main reason for going to see a regression therapist was because he felt uneasy during business discussions, and he felt the danger of losing his job if he was not able to achieve the minimum turn over. When Dr. Goldberg asked him specific questions he told him that he has always allowed himself to be dominated and used by his relatives, acquaintances and friends. This caused him great suffering. Dr. Goldberg put Arnold into a trance and led him back to the root of his problem, which he was able to trace back to a previous life. I will now tell you Arnold's answers to Dr. Goldberg's questions during regression.

"I am lying under a table... That's where I eat... I am chained to the table by my hands and feet... My master has chained me up.. I am his apprentice... He is a gold and silversmith. His name is master Gustav... My name is Theuer. I live in a small town in Bavaria. It is the year 1132. After I've finished work in the workshop he always chains me to the table, so that I don't run away. He hates me. He beats me with a whip. I am afraid of him. He gets satisfaction from putting me down and causing me pain. He also abuses me sexually... An elegant young woman called Klothilde often visits the workshop to order jewellery for her family. She seems to be interested in me, for she always asks after me. Master

Gustav tells her that I am good for nothing. As soon as she has left he beats me again... Now she is asking my master to allow me to come to her house in order to repair something there. Master Gustav tells her that I can't be trusted. I am angry... I am a lot bigger and stronger now. He is about to chain me to the table again. I resist him for the first time. I am so angry. I want to kill him. I grab a tool to hit him with. We wrestle with each other. I try to suffocate him with my hands. He just laughs at me. Now he pushes me away and grabs a big knife. He stabs it into my stomach again and again... I am floating above my body. I feel no more pain..."

18 months after Arnold's regression a lawyer walks into Dr. Goldberg's practice. This man he calls Brian in his book. Brian wishes to experience a past life. He had heard a lot about regression therapy and was curious to find out more. Dr. Goldberg then discovers that this man is a very successful lawyer. Everything seems to go his way since he has the ability to twist people around his fingers. He admitted to having a problem. He suffers from sleeplessness and is plagued by a bad conscience of having shamelessly used people for his own ends. When asked about his hobbies, he admitted to having a passion for collecting hand crafted items made of gold and silver.

After having put his client into a trance Dr. Goldberg tried to discover the root cause of Brian's present-day problems in a past life. When the so-called *scanning* of his present-day life only revealed some minor events but not the root cause, Dr. Goldberg lead his client into a past life hoping it would shed light on his present-day problems. Soon his client saw himself in a past life, and responding to the therapist's intermittent questions, Bryan reported the following:

"I work in a workshop. I am a gold and silversmith – a very good one. My name is Gustav. I live in Bavaria. The year is 1130..."Dr. Goldberg could not believe his ears. He had already heard about this Bavarian goldsmith somewhere. Who had told him about this? He had had so many clients coming to his practice wanting to relive their past lives. Which one had told him about a goldsmith? Back to questioning his client:

"No I am not married...Two popes have recently been chosen. Everyone is talking about it." (Dr. Goldberg later found this to be the truth. Two popes really had been ordained in 1130 AD.)

Next the regression therapist asked his client who was still in trance, "Whom did you hate most in your life?" "My apprentice Theuer. He is good for nothing..." Dr. Goldberg felt cold shivers run down his spine. He now remembered Arnold who had been stabbed to death by the master goldsmith Gustav. Could it really be true that here on the couch lies the murderer? Well, I can find no other explanation. When questioned about hating his apprentice the Goldsmith answered, "I just hate him. I seem to gain satisfaction from torturing him." [23] This man's voice was much deeper than Brian's. He also talked faster. His way of thinking was gruesome, mean, sadistic, for he continued saying, "I am far too good to this lad... Of course I beat him. He deserves nothing better... My business is thriving thanks to my skills, but no thanks to that useless lad. He's always thinking about that young lady..Klothilde... She is the daughter of a wealthy family and this good for nothing imagines that she's interested in him who is such an ordinary person. Anyway, the boy is my property. Then this Klothilde has the cheek to ask me whether she can take Theuer home, so that he can mend something for her. Why does she not ask me? After all I am the master and far more skilled. After she had left I decided to give this lad the biggest hiding he has ever had in his life. I want to chain him up again. But this insolent lad suddenly resists me. He throws himself at me and we fall to the floor. I laugh at his pathetic attempts to injury me. I hit him and he grabs my throat. In my anger I throw him against the wall. Now I grab my knife and stab it into his stomach......."

What do you make of that? Imagine having been Dr. Goldberg who suddenly received this information about the same events from two different clients. Would this not have sent shivers down your spine? Dr. Goldberg is convinced that Brian and Arnold have never met or heard of each other in this life. He thinks it no coincidence that he should experience this synchronicity of events in his practice, brought to him from two different sources. If you were to calculate the probability of such an event happening twice in the Middle Ages, the ratio would be something like one to a few billion. He dismissed any dishonesty. If we were dealing with some carefully rigged prank this would have been obvious from the start.

Dr. Goldberg did not want to play God and did not introduce the two men to each other. As he says, "If these two people were meant to meet in this life, then this meeting would be arranged by a higher force." Arnold had also told him during regression that Klothilde was his sister-in-law in his present life, and the one whom he gets along best with, out of all the people he knows. When Arnold was asked about Gustav, he answered that he was unable to find him in his present life.

PROOF OF REINCARNATION THROUGH GROUP REGRESSION

Most popular of all are my group regressions, which I have been leading since the mid-eighties in this country and abroad. Those taking part bring blankets and pillows. After an introduction they are given the theme which will be used in the following regression. This is always a theme, which applies to everyone present. Such themes may be entitled, *'My most beautiful past life,' 'My most spiritual past life,' 'My most meaningful past life,' 'My previous past life,' 'My most wonderful life as the opposite sex,'* and so on. There are a great number of themes available that could easily apply to everyone.

During a regression such as this, which lasts about an hour, 70% - 90% of participants will experience their past lives, each person experiencing his own. Only at the end of the session does everyone have a chance to share their experiences with the group. In group regression I make use of a countdown relaxation method, whereas in individual regressions I tend to use hypnosis. Both achieve the required Alpha state of mind in order to project images relating to past lives onto the inner monitor. These images are stored in the subconscious in the right hand side of the brain. If a very deep Alpha state is reached, the events from a past life will be experienced as vividly as daily life in the present. All senses and feelings will be experienced simultaneously. It is really an incredible experience to have undergone this, whether as an individual or in a group. In group regressions, as opposed to regression therapy, we never delve into traumatic events; firstly, so that there is no backlog left to deal with afterwards and secondly, because this creates less disturbance during group sessions. Should anyone in the group relive a traumatic experience he might start shaking and screaming which would bring the others out of the past and back into the present.

In the Saxon town of Halle such a group regression was being held using the theme: 'A beautiful life as the opposite sex.' A journalist for one of the largest German newspapers experienced himself as his own grandmother who had died at the age of 22. His experience was so vivid and real that this regression was quite an experience for him. He had known very little about his Grandmother other than the fact that she had died young. His grandfather's sister was still alive, so he was able to question her about what he had seen and experienced. She was amazed at how he could have known all those details about her sister's childhood, youth and married life. She confirmed everything he told her. He accurately described the sewing machine, which his grandmother had used, remembering that it had an intricate pattern on the top of the treadle. The family had not kept the sewing machine, so the journalist could not have seen it before. For him this was proof of reincarnation.

During a group regression into a spiritual life, a woman in Switzerland claimed to have seen herself as a Benedictine monk in Italy about 500 years ago. The man on the mat next to her, who was a total stranger, had apparently also been a monk named Domenico at the same monastery. When she told him he replied, "Yes, I too saw myself in that monastery. You were the Abbot." After the seminar they both sat together for a long time describing what they had seen and experienced during regression. The following year they travelled to Italy together to find the monastery. When they got there they were told that it had been demolished long ago. These two monks from the past have been living together as partners for some years now.

It is not unusual in my experience for participants to discover during regression that someone else taking part had shared a previous life with them. In this way friendships or even partnerships are often renewed having lain dormant for hundreds of years. At one time three marriages evolved out of one regression seminar. One of the women is now an opera singer.

Two people who attended one of my seminars 25 years ago and became close friends. From that time onwards they have been telephoning each other every day. Sometimes it happens that they both buy exactly the same thing at exactly the same time, even though they live 300 kilometres apart. They have never fallen out with each other or experienced jealousy regarding men. They often go for walks hugging each other, but have no lesbian relationship. Though both have been married since.

During my seminar they discovered to their amazement that they had both been knights in the Middle Ages. Each of them separately saw themselves as the others twin brother in knights' armour. They spoke of having had the same experiences as their twin, who during regression was discovered to be their closest friend in the present. One of the women had been given a staff bearing a cross by her spirit guide the day before the weekend seminar. She was told she would soon find out the meaning of this. She then told us that during regression she had seen the knight holding the staff in his hand.

In my group regressions, participants are asked to choose someone they know as their subject, and most love to choose a friend or relative to find out which lives they have shared in the past. Everyone chooses a person 'A'. For example, a young woman chose her mother as person 'A'. She experienced three lives with her. When she got home after the seminar she told her mother nothing about her experiences other than the fact that she had seen her in three different lives. The daughter then encouraged her mother to attend one of Trutz Hardo's seminars and to choose her as person 'A'. They wanted to check whether they would see themselves in the same lives. Her mother attended the following group regression in Berlin. The daughter later told me on the phone that her mother had remembered two of the same lives and that the people and situations had matched the other's descriptions. Independent of each other they had made sketches of their houses and the interior layout in order to compare them. These drawings matched perfectly. This was convincing evidence of reincarnation for both of them.

During a seminar in Munich I felt a shiver down my spine. Without previously having decided anything, a couple chose each other as person 'A'. When it came to sharing their experiences the man said that he had chosen his wife as person 'A'. She had been his mother in a previous incarnation. They lived in a village near Nurnberg in the year 1845. His father had died, and he was her only child. His name was Karl. Twice a week they had gone to the market in Nurnberg to sell fruit and vegetables. Suddenly the woman sitting next to him at the seminar shouts at him saying, "Stop! Stop! I have seen the same thing. You wear my Karlchen!" When she had calmed down a bit she described exactly what she had experienced as Karl's mother at that time. She could confirm everything her husband had told about this past life.

Wouldn't you have had shivers down your spine had you been present at this seminar? There is one more experience I must tell you about. At a regression seminar in which I lead the group into their previous lives, one of the women saw herself as a pilot who was shot down during the bombings over Berlin. She described what she had experienced in great detail. Then she said, "My name was Phillip Morris." I thought, "How stupid, maybe she didn't reach a deep alpha state and had invented this." Everyone present must have had similar thoughts, for this was a well-known brand of cigarettes. But this woman insisted that that had been her name. She was absolutely certain of it. She even knew his date of birth and the date he died. Several months later she took a walk with her husband along the Havel in Berlin. On their way back they happened to pass the cemetery in Heer St. where the British soldiers were buried. She said to her husband, "I have this feeling that my body was buried here. Let's go and have a look. Maybe we'll find something." At the entrance was a list of all the British soldiers who had died in the Second World War. She then discovered the name of Phillip Morris bearing the exact dates of his birth and death, which she already knew from having remembered it through regression.

For those unable to take part in an individual or group regression, or for others seeking to discover more about their past lives, I suggest buying yourself CDs with which you can safely explore your past lives in your own time.

A PSYCHOLOGIST'S EVIDENCE OF REINCARNATION

Are all memories of past lives experienced by those taking part in group regression seminars real events from another time? Do the individuals involved embellish their stories? Is it not true that many people see themselves as having been someone famous in history? Is not every other person claiming to have been the likes of Nofretitis, Cleopatra, Julius Caesar, Alexander the Great, Napoleon or Emperor Sissi? A psychologist in the United States wanted to find out whether there was any truth in such regressions, or whether she could prove that all such memories were only wishful thinking or fantasy. These images from our subconscious could mistakenly lead us to believe that these experiences really happened in the past. This professor lecturing at Berkeley University in California is called Helen Wambach.

In 1981 I went to visit her at her workplace situated in the remote mountains of Oakland. I asked her to lead me into one of my past lives, since I had never experienced this before. I had read several books on regression therapy, but the actual experience was still to come. In this first regression I saw myself as a woman with long dark hair in a pink dress. I was about 20 years old. I was deeply unhappy gazing out of a window of a small castle. Spread out in front of me was a rather overgrown park like garden. Then I saw myself sitting at the dinner table. Opposite me sat my stepmother who was barely 40. I could feel her coldness towards me. On my right sat my father's brother. He was holding a lamb chop in his left hand and the fat was dripping down his arm. He was eating very noisily, gorging himself most horribly. I shuddered in disgust. At the head of the table next to my uncle sat my father. I felt a deep, warm connection and trust towards him. He seemed to be my only consolation in that life.

When I returned from that life which I had lived in France in 1204, we discussed the experiences I had just been through. I was amazed at the images and even more so at the intensity of my feelings. When I think back on my memories of my present life, I also see images in my mind but these are generally not accompanied by feelings. It was a completely new way of experiencing the past for me. It was all so real and familiar and yet completely different then a film. Even so it was not enough proof for me. Helen then invited me to dinner in a restaurant and explained much about her methods that served to prove the truth of reincarnation. She thought that the truth of what is experienced during regression could only be proven statistically. A single regression may be enough evidence for the person involved, but for objective evidence we would need more than that. If she was to take a 1000 people into regression and ask them specific questions relating to the time and the world in which they had once lived, they would surely come up with certain facts which would be the same for all of them.

Helen decided to do this by leading 1088 people into their past lives and asking them about their age, race, career, clothes, country and also things like, "Look at the money. What does it look like?" or "What kind of cutlery are you using?" When questioned, most citizens of the USA said they would like to be reborn as white males. The statistics based on those who went into past life regression showed that throughout history the male to female ratio has always been 50:50 with a slight increase of males from time to time of 0.3- 0.6%. These results were consistent even when 75% of the people involved in the regressions were female. Therefore, if the experiences during regression were based on wishful thinking, then most white Americans undergoing regression therapy would see themselves as white men. This proved not to be the case; most of them were very simple people in their past lives with all variations of skin colours. Out of these 1088 people involved in this experiment who each relived many past lives — all in all approximately 10,000 lives — only one person saw himself as a famous historical person, one other member saw himself as an anonymous king, and several claimed to have been high priests. All the other lives experienced at various times in history revealed a ratio between upper, middle and lower class, which proved to be exactly the same as the statistics which the economists and cultural historians came up with. According to these historical statistics approximately 75% of the world's population belongs to the lower class. They are farmers, fishermen, soldiers, beggars and the like. Approximately 20% belong to the middle-class, which consists mostly of craftsmen and tradesmen. The rest, the so-called upper class, includes all those who have no need to work due to power, land ownership or wealth. This group is made up of about 5% of all people. The people accessed during regression were exactly divided into these ratios. It is certainly not true that every other person was Cleopatra, Napoleon, Caesar or the like. I could only prove this by having observed and recorded over 10,000 past life accounts during regression.

One of the many questions that Helen Wambach put to her clients during these experiments was about the money used at that particular time in history. For example, those that had lived between 400 BC and 40 years after Christ saw rectangular coins with a hole in the middle. No one among those in regression knew that such coins existed in those days. When asked about clothes they described exactly those worn at that time in history. No one mentioned having worn trousers at any time before the year 1200. These were only just coming into fashion at this time. Similarly no one mentioned eating with a fork before the year 1500. During

the 300 years after that only a three pronged fork was used
in Europe. There were no historical differences between
these dates. To my amazement no one mentioned a four-
pronged fork before the year 1790. The people in regression
could not have known these historically correct facts. Did
you know when a three or four pronged fork first appeared
in Europe? [24]

For many people interested in reincarnation, Helen
Wambach's investigations revealed the most convincing
evidence. But as you are about to be shown even more
convincing evidence was about to emerge.

Having dealt mainly with group regressions in the past two
chapters, it is now time to return to individual regressions.
I want to begin with a case that caused great upheaval in
the USA during the 1950's and helped to bring reincarnation into the open.

BRIDEY MURPHY STIRS
AMERICA'S EMOTIONS

On the 29th November 1952 Morey Bernstein, an amateur
hypnotist from Pueblo in Colorado, hypnotised a 29 year-
old woman called Virginia Tighe Morrow. This took place
at his home in the presence of her husband. Bernstein had
never led anyone back into a past life, but thought Virginia
would be an excellent candidate for his first try after having

met her at a group regression. He led her back through her childhood and her time in the womb and further back in time. "Allow yourself to go further and further back in time, back, back, back until you see a landscape and experience a different time and place. Now see if you can describe the images you see."

Client: I am scratching the paint off my bed. It has just only been painted nicely. It's an iron bed. I am scratching the paint off. My fingernails have already ruined both bedposts. It looks terrible.

Bernstein: Why did you do that?

Client: I don't know. I was crazy. I got beaten for it.

Bernstein: What's your name?

Client: Bridey.

Bernstein: Do you have another name?

Client: Bridey Murphy.

Bernstein: And where do you live?

Client: I live in Cork.

Bernstein: What's your mother's name?

Client: Kathleen.

Bernstein: And what's your father's name?

Client: Duncan.... Duncan... Murphy.

Bernstein: How old are you?

Client: Four... four years old.

This is how the first of six sessions began, which later caused uproar in America. Virginia (pseudonym Ruth Simmons in Bernstein's book) claims to have been born on the 20th December 1798 as Bridget Kathleen Murphy. Her father had been a solicitor and they had lived outside Cork in *The Meadows*. She told him the name of her teacher. At the age of 20 she had married Sean McCarthy who was a Catholic. They had moved to Belfast together, where he once more worked as a solicitor. They had remained childless and she had died in 1864 after falling down the stairs. She describes many incidents from her youth and her life in Belfast as well as exact descriptions of her neighbourhood, her neighbours, the layout of the streets etc.

Suddenly she began to sing some old Irish folk songs which were popular in those days. The interesting thing was the fact that neither Virginia nor Morey Bernstein had ever been to Ireland, or had read any books about the country.

Three issues of the Denver Post, which was a rather popular paper, contained reports about this case, which amazed many of its readers. Until now nothing had been mentioned publicly about the possibility of regression into past lives. A well-known publishing company now encouraged Morey Bernstein to write a book about these six sessions with Virginia. On the 1st January 1956 it was published causing great excitement and later becoming a bestseller. The Denver Post sent its reporter William J. Barker to Ireland where he was able to prove many of Virginia's claims with the help of local bibliographers and historians. Virginia had mentioned two grocery stores and the names of the owners William Farr and John Carrigan, which were both traced. Likewise, the suburb she had called *The Meadows* was found on an old map, but a place she had called *Mourne* was only found much later by a historian. She had said that her father in-law John McCarthy had been a solicitor in Cork. This too could be proven. During regression the person calling herself Bridey Murphy described some Irish traditions relating to that time. At weddings it was traditional to put money into the bride's pockets. She mentioned that she had kissed the *Blarney Stone*, an ancient heathen custom, which is no longer common in this century. Several scientists thought she was just making it all up. Sometime later one of the bibliographers by the name of Dermot Foley apologised to her, after finding a description of those customs in an old book. People tried to tell her that iron beds did not exist at that time, but even this, like so many other things, was later proven to have been correct.

When some Irish speech specialists heard the recorded voice of Bridey Murphy they were surprised at how genuine her strong regional Irish accent sounded. She also used many commonly used words of that time, which today have long been forgotten. Likewise, her descriptions of traditional celebrations and the songs sung at such occasions, aroused much amazement. Whenever the truth was questioned regarding certain idioms or a reference to folklore, Bridey Murphy was always proved right. How could she have spoken so perfectly in the Irish dialect dating back a hundred years from the region she claimed to have lived in?

A dispute developed among many of America's newspapers, since the Randolph-Hearst chain of papers tried everything to discredit Bridey Murphy by consciously publishing half-truths. Other papers backed the Denver Post, which examined the case and then published their findings. The story of Bridey Murphy aroused strong feelings in millions of people and the interest in reincarnation rose rapidly. Since scientists and other enthusiasts were now getting to grips with reincarnation and were conducting private regressions, America soon became the leading country on the subject of past lives.

Apart from this it may be of some interest to mention that Mrs. Virginia Tighe had not believed in reincarnation. She died in 1995 at the age of 72. In 1976 the Los Angeles Times had questioned her about how she felt about having been Bridey Murphy in hindsight. She answered, "I had been brought up not to believe in reincarnation. Research is showing us that it exists, but I must be convinced of the truth in my own experience. I am an open-minded person and to me it makes more sense for God to have a plan that knows no boundaries. My whole life I have been taught to keep God fenced in, yet I have since decided to believe that there is more to life than we can imagine." [25]

THE MASSACRE OF JEWS IN YORK

Doctor Arnold Bloxham lived in Wales in the 1920's and became well known through his work with hypnotism, which he used in the presence of his dentist to help patients experience pain free treatment, even during tooth extractions. Later he became famous through a TV programme regarding his work as a regression sex therapist. In these live shows he led people into past lives on television.

One of these clients was a housewife called Jane Evans, whom he had previously taken back into seven of her past lives. The most dramatic of these was one in which her name was Rebecca, the wife of a bank manager called Joseph who had settled with his family in York. Rebecca described the fear they felt as Jews in 1190, as citizens like themselves were treated with hostility. There had been protests against the Jews since 200 Christians had died during a plague in the past year, but not one Jew had been infected. They were blamed for having poisoned the well and were forced to wear a yellow disc on their chest as a mark of identification. The new King Richard the Lion heart had recently set out for the Holy Land on a crusade to free Jerusalem from Christ's enemies. Meanwhile in his homeland, many people including the priest's were pointing a finger at the Jews. They knew that they were non-believers, and therefore enemies of Christ, and had allowed their saviour to be killed. Rebecca described how the fear set in among the Jews in York. They barricaded their houses from the inside, but later thought it best to flee. Anti-Jew protests seemed to be springing up everywhere, and the word spread that 30 Jews had been murdered in London.

In mid-March the following happened; several men led by the Royal Marbelise broke into the houses of the Jews. Marbelise owed Joseph a lot of money and had hoped to free himself of this debt by murdering him. The Jews managed to escape to the castle where they had been promised protection, but when they arrived there the castle warden only opened the outside gate keeping the actual gates to the castle closed. They were trapped between the inner and outer walls of the castle. They could not get in or out and were unable to find food or water. They remained there several days while the mob tried to break down the outer gate shouting: "Kill the Jews!" Since the prisoners knew that it was only a matter of time before the bloodthirsty mob would break in and massacre them all, they killed each other. First the children, then the women and finally the men. The same tragedy later occurred in Worms and Mainz.

Joseph had managed to bribe someone from the castle to show him a secret passage that led him and his family outside the town gates. The family hid in a nearby Church, where Joseph and his son took the priest and the verger prisoner. They hid there hoping that the mob as well as the inhabitants of the castle would not discover them. From the Church tower they could see their houses burning. They had not eaten for days and so both father and son risked leaving the church in order to find food, disguising themselves so as not to be recognised. During their absence Rebecca heard the sound of horses approaching, then voices, from which she could tell that they were searching for them. They thought the Church to be a likely hiding place. She hid herself and her daughter in a crypt below the altar. The priest who had been freed by the horseman knew where Rebecca and Rachel were hiding and had informed the murderers of their whereabouts. These men soon found their way into the crypt where they murdered Rebecca and her daughter.

While she was recounting this she experienced everything just as it had happened in her past. You could hear the fear in her voice. She screamed, "Please spare Rachel's life, please, please spare her!"

Whoever has had the chance to witness such a dramatic regression will know that it is definitely not imagination, unless of course your client was one of the world's best actors. The interesting thing about this case was that during the research the church was found but had no crypt under the altar. That particular Church was later converted into a museum. During the conversions the crypt in which Rebecca and her daughter had died was discovered, making this case extremely valid as evidence of reincarnation.

The recordings of Rebecca's descriptions of these events were shown to a well-known local historian Professor Dobson, who agreed that her account was accurate regarding the events and the time at which they occurred. He was extremely impressed by her detailed accounts of some of these events. Several of the as yet unresolved references may well have been as she had remembered them, but the historical data is only accessible to scientists specialising in historical research.

Even if Mrs. Evans had previously read books about the massacre, she could never have gained such detailed knowledge and could not have known about the crypt. Most of this information has not even been published and is stored in archives to which only historians have access. It was also impossible for her to have picked up this information telepathically from Dr. Bloxham's thoughts, since he had no knowledge of the events that occurred at that time.

Dr. Bloxham gives us some evidence that substantiates the fact that relived events are real by claiming the following, "I asked various people after hypnosis about the recently relived events that were still fresh in their minds. Their facts were substantially different to anything they could have read about in history books. When I tried to give them facts which I knew to be correct according to my historical knowledge but which differed from those experienced by them during hypnosis, my clients would always claim that the facts I was giving them were false."[26] In many cases the truth could only be verified later by researching archive material.

As a regression therapist I have often had similar experiences at my practice, but don't always have the time to find out whether all the facts are historically correct. Since I have studied history I usually know whether the facts that the person in trance comes up with correspond to those in the history books. When I question people about the historical period that they have just relived, I often discover that they knew practically nothing about that particular time in history. Most of these people were very simple folks in their past life, mostly uneducated and with little interest in politics or events taking place in the rest of the world. They were only able to talk about these historical events related to the suffering they experienced in that life. I will tell you more about this after the next story that was broadcast on television on the 21ˢᵗ April 1994.

THE RETURN OF A MUCH-LOVED MOTHER

Jeffrey is an only child born of Jewish parents and grew up in New York with them. He went to a regression therapist Jeanne Avery because he was suffering from depression. He told her he had fears of the future, in particular a fear of unexpected events. He tended to trust no one. During regression it was revealed that his entire childhood had been shrouded in sadness. His father had loved his mother above everyone. During the thirties she had remained in her homeland, though her son had begged her to leave Nazi

Germany as quickly as possible, since the Jews there were in more danger as each day passed. He even sent her money. His mother wrote to him saying that she had not given up hope yet and wanted to stay for now. But then it was too late. Soon it became impossible to leave Germany if you were Jewish, and rumours and news spread of the horrors to which the Jews were subjected.

His mother had not survived the Holocaust and he never really discovered what happened to her. Jeffrey's father was convinced that she met her death in the gas chambers along with millions of others. Jeffrey's father fostered feelings of guilt thinking he should have tried harder at the time to take his mother out of Germany and over to America. It had become impossible for him to enjoy his life knowing his mother had lost her life in such a gruesome way. All laughter and all the joy left his house. A time of deep mourning began and everyone else in the family was expected to grieve with him.

Jeanne Avery writes, "On the one hand Jeffrey felt love and closeness towards his father, but on the other he could not understand why he should spend his entire life grieving for someone he had never known. He felt he had been robbed of a normal childhood and youth since this dark cloud of mourning hung over everything. He also felt that his father was barely conscious of his son's existence and because of this he came to the conclusion that his father did not love him. Finally he was convinced that he would only receive his loving attention if he himself died."

During his regression into the childhood of his present life it was discovered that Jeffrey had been almost totally ignored. It made no difference how cute, charming or intelligent he was for his age, he could not win his father's love. This was kept for his mother who had died some time ago. He would never be able to replace her. During regression Jeffrey suddenly saw himself as a woman who lived near Berlin on her own. She was very content with her life. Her husband had died some years ago. She had a son who lived in New York and had visited him there. But she could not stand being there for long. She longed for her home, her close friends and neighbours. In the late thirties her son repeatedly demanded that she come and live near him in America. But she was optimistic by nature and tried to allay his fears. She had also written to him telling him that several soldiers were living with Jewish families who were very friendly towards them. Many foodstuffs were becoming increasingly hard to come by and she had cultivated vegetables and potatoes in her garden.

Meanwhile the correspondence with her son in America had long ended due to the war. She heard from her Jewish neighbours that they had started to bury their silver and jewellery in their gardens. They feared being asked to leave very suddenly and being given only minutes to pack their belongings. Nonetheless, this woman always remained optimistic. One day a German soldier even brought her some chocolate. When the restrictions were imposed on the Jews it was always said to be for their own safety.

One day she really was called on to pack very quickly, and was to leave her house for several weeks. The soldiers she had become acquainted with were no longer friendly; in fact they behaved as if they no longer knew her. Many Jews, including children, were now loaded onto lorries. These were so overcrowded that many of them had nowhere to sit. The children began to cry. Nothing had been organised for such events, and they were given no food or drink. Finally they arrived at buildings like sheds into which they were crammed. Several families had to share a room measuring a few square metres. Only now the woman realised how naive she had been not to have listened to the pleas of her son asking her to go to America as soon as possible. The German guards were anything but friendly. If any of the Jews demanded anything or complained, they were shot immediately. There were far too few toilets and those that were available were broken. An unbelievable stench spread through the place. Everyone was hungry, thirsty and freezing with cold. The babies screamed non-stop because they were hungry. After several weeks they were once more loaded onto lorries. When they finally stopped after a very long journey they were taken to an entrance hall to a large shower room in which new clothing was stacked up in piles. They were told that they must first shower before putting the new clothes on. But instead of the anticipated shower, gas streamed out of the showerheads and everyone died a gruesome death.

When Jeffrey returned to his present-day consciousness he

had plenty more to tell, "I was reborn very soon after. I was my father's mother. I desperately wanted to return to my son by being born as his son, to show him that I was still alive and well and that I am still with him. But how could I explain to my father that I am his mother who has returned? This is even difficult for me to grasp." After a pause he continued, "I can see clearly now why I came back; I wanted to give my father as much love and attention as possible."

Jeffrey reassured his regression therapist that he has never read reports of the holocaust or watched films about it. He simply had no interest in it. People had talked endlessly about his grandmother so he had no wish to hear any more. He also said that what he had just experienced could not have been read about or imagined. It had to have surfaced from his subconscious into his conscious mind.[27]

Thousands of Jews like the Chassids, the Kabbalists, as well as many esoterically interested people believe in reincarnation. Many of them suffer from nightmares possibly related to the Holocaust, or from other symptoms such as asthma, weight problems, depression, claustrophobia or panic attacks when hearing of these times, or when confronted by films dealing with this subject. A large number of these people find their way to regression therapists. This usually helps them to find the cause of their problems, which are often rooted in their past lives. The mere insight into the origin of these disturbing symptoms can in itself lessen or even dissolve them. There are many Jewish regression therapists in the United States. Regression therapists are offered advanced courses in which they are taught how to effectively help clients who were the victims of the Holocaust in a past life. I myself have been able to free many Jewish and non-Jewish people who in their previous lives were confronted with this gloomy chapter in the history of mankind. As I see it, successful regression therapy provides us with the strongest evidence for reincarnation. This is why, my dear readers, I wish to tell you a little more about it in the following chapter.

EVIDENCE OF REINCARNATION REVEALED THROUGH REGRESSION THERAPY

Regression, i.e. Reincarnation therapy, opens the way for a client to connect with his Higher Self and to receive spiritual guidance. It enables him to immerse himself in his subconscious or his emotional body and to reach the storage chamber of the past. This is where the origins of his present symptoms of disturbance such as fears, phobias, obsessions, depressions, allergies, sleeplessness, chronic pains, migraines, asthma, nightmares, relationship problems and many others are stored. Through this we have discovered that the majority of such unpleasant symptoms originate in past lives. Problems in the present life are often markers or side effects of the original causes. If one uncovers the original cause and dissolves the emotions and programming which have been lodged in the subconscious, namely in the emotional body, then such disturbing symptoms can often be dissolved in a single therapy session. The healing potential through regression therapy is enormous. The research in reincarnation has made this beneficial therapy possible for mankind.

I want to give you a few brief examples of my work so that you can picture this therapy in a little more detail. A woman came to me who since her earliest childhood had had problems with her mother. This mother seemed to ignore her daughter totally, or pushed her away from her, while being happy to have her other children on her lap. During regression therapy it emerged that the client had been an attractive Viennese woman about 220 years ago, who had fallen in love with a well-respected and wealthy man. This man returned her love but marriage was an unthinkable prospect, since he was married and a divorce from his wife was out of question for religious and social reasons. This Viennese woman had poisoned her lover's wife with his consent. The wife who had been poisoned is now, as you might have guessed her present mother. During regression therapy my client was asked to offer a chalice containing a liquid of love, forgiveness, and ingredients intended to dissipate sorrow and guilt to the wife who had been poisoned in the past. She handed her this chalice and asked her for forgiveness. Following that she imagined offering the chalice to her present mother and in doing so asks her for forgiveness too.

You, dear readers, can surely imagine why this mother today unconsciously reacted to her daughter the way she did. All our behaviour is borne out of the sum of our past experiences and feelings, even when these stretch back a long way in time.

This story has not ended yet. When this woman got home after her therapy session the telephone rang. It was her mother on line. It was the first time she had called her daughter since the daughter had left her parent's house 25 years before. She said, "My love" (all her life she had never been able to bring herself to use words like that towards her daughter.) "I know that you wish to travel to America next summer. I happen to have an American coming to visit me tomorrow afternoon. Please join us for tea at four o'clock so that I can introduce you to this gentleman. He is likely to have a lot of information that may be of interest to you." The following day her mother opened the door to her daughter, hugged her, took her hand and introduced her to her American visitor. Her behaviour towards her daughter had completely changed. Do you know why? This change in behaviour occurred because her daughter had begged her mother to forgive her for this gruesome crime. This act of forgiveness during therapy worked long distance. The mother's subconscious had registered her daughter's plea for forgiveness and had granted it.

Here are some more examples.

A man who had been married for 20 years confided in me that he wished to find out why his wife has rejected him sexually ever since they were married. It turned out that he had raped this woman when he was a soldier approximately 200 years ago. Unbeknown to her, her subconscious, namely her emotional body, was resisting being touched sexually by her previous rapist. During therapy he offered her the chalice of forgiveness and asked to be forgiven. The following morning the man looked me up and told me that he had spent his first sexually satisfying night with his wife. He had told her nothing about what went on during therapy. Once more the woman's subconscious had sensed her husband's plea for forgiveness from far away and she had granted it. You can imagine how many shaky marriages could possibly be healed by means of regression therapy.

A young mother suffered from an urge to drink one or two litres of water every morning before taking her children to the nursery. Her legs above the ankles were swollen heavily and the prescribed medication was of no use. During regression she saw herself approximately 200 years ago as the leader of a caravan whose job it was to lead all the people safely across the desert. He had told his companions that they only needed to take enough water for ten days. They would then have reached an oasis where they would find plenty to drink. When they arrived there ten days later, they discovered that the oasis had been completely covered with sand. Needless to say they all died of thirst. The final programming which this caravan leader laid down for himself before he died was, "I will never leave home with too little water again." This programming has been working itself out over many lives and was still present now in her life as a young mother. We immediately dissolved this programming which had been damaging her present life so severely. The following day she told me that after her therapy session she had had to pass water every 20 minutes. She also proudly added, "I left my house without having to drink water today, and look! My legs are back to normal after all these years. The water has drained out of them."

People who cannot bear to wear anything tight around their necks such as roll neck jumpers, bow ties, shirt collars etc., are likely to have suffered injuries to the neck in a past life, died by suffocation, hanging, strangling or were possibly beheaded. People who cannot stand wearing a watch on their wrists are likely to have been tied up by these with ropes or chains in a previous life. Whenever they feel restricted in this area it reminds them unconsciously and involuntarily of unpleasant situations in their past causing aversions to similar restrictions. Most allergies can be traced back to negative experiences. If someone died of choking on a fish bone, eating a poisoned apple or poisonous mushrooms, they will often develop an allergy to fish, apples or mushrooms in their present lives. In my regression therapy I have often experienced that clients who suffer from being overweight, starved to death in a previous life and programmed themselves at the time by saying things like, "I never want to be hungry again." Unconsciously these people are subject to such programming from their past, until it is dissolved during regression therapy. I believe that this form of therapy will also come to be accepted scientifically and could completely revolutionise the medical world, psychology and psychotherapy. These discoveries demand that reincarnation become accepted for what it is. I could give you dozens of similar examples of spontaneous results that have occurred during my regression therapy.

But now it is time to turn our attention to the most convincing and no longer undeniable proof of reincarnation. The hard evidence that has recently come to light through hypnosis will be outshone by a case recently investigated by the famous Dr. Bruce Goldberg. During the nineties this case once again stirred America's emotions, just as the case of Bridey Murphy did in the Fifties. Television broadcast the news throughout the world, and even a film was made with the title *Search for Grace*. The book by Dr. Goldberg, bearing the same title, promptly became a best seller after that. This may well be the most effectively documented and hence the most convincing evidence of reincarnation that has ever been publicly released.

In the second half of the 20th Century California is breaking the mould and heralding a new era of spiritual discovery and a new awareness and understanding of ancient knowledge and wisdom. This is happening in the field of psychology, spiritual psychology, in regression therapy and also in reincarnation therapy. Great eastern masters such as Yogananda, Vivekananda, Muktananda, and many others, who in the Sixties had already fully blossomed, had sown the seeds of this in the first half of the 20th Century. Today we are able to reap the harvest of this era. I am convinced that the fruits born of this spiritual seed will influence our whole way of thinking in the future.

SEARCH FOR GRACE

In 1987 Dr. Bruce Goldberg received a phone call from a woman in her thirties called Ivy who explained that she has twice seen him on television. This encouraged her to pick up the phone and arrange an appointment for regression therapy. When she came to his practice in Baltimore she gave him the impression of being polite and rather shy. Her reason for coming to see him was to find out why she has such a destructive relationship with her friend John, who abuses her physically and psychologically and had almost killed her three times. John was insincere, unpredictable and egoistic. Nonetheless, she could not let him go. She was quick to forgive his behaviour and his brutality after he promised her each time that it would never happen again. At the same time Ivy felt drawn to another man who seemed to be the total opposite of John. He was polite, loving, trustworthy, and had not had much experience with women.

Ivy's dilemma was that she was fond of both men, valuing Dave's sincere and deep love, and yet not being able to give up her passionate addiction to John. Everything pointed towards a decision in favour of Dave, but still she could not let go of John. On top of all this she was plagued by nightmares in which a man repeatedly murdered her. She had the feeling that it was John even though he looked completely different and wore different clothes. She suffered from sleeplessness, since after nightmares like that it was difficult to go back to sleep. She then feared going to sleep in case she was subjected to more disturbing dreams.

After 45 sessions she was healed of her destructive relationship with John and was having a fulfilling relationship with Dave. Many other problems that came up during therapy were also successfully dealt with. She had gained her self-confidence, her nightmares had vanished and she could once again sleep peacefully. In numerous lives John had murdered her in various guises and different times. In most of these lives Dave had been the *good friend* who wanted to save her. If we bring the law of Karma into this, which states that we draw to ourselves that which we once inflicted on others, then Ivy must have behaved in a most murderous fashion committing some terrible deeds in previous lives.

Dr. Goldberg saw her regression therapy as complete, but Ivy reminded him of her phobia of not being able to swallow. No one was permitted to touch her throat either, not even

Dave, and she could not bear to wear anything restricting around her neck. Ivy and her therapist agreed that this symptom, being the last of many, must be dealt with and dissolved as before. They never imagined that this regression they were about to go into would make history and contribute to the evidence of reincarnation in a big way. Dr. Goldberg recorded the entire session and also kept notes as usual.

During regression she suddenly saw herself back in the year 1925. Her name was Grace Doze; and she was 31 years old. She was having an argument with Chester her husband. He was an employee of General Electric. They had a one-year-old son by the name of Cliff. He often stayed with Grace's mother in the same village. Her husband accused her of having affairs with other men. When Dr. Goldberg asked her whether this was true, she admitted it was and said that her *idiot* of a husband did not know how to make her happy. She was in the prime of her life, attractive and could not envisage herself being faithful. Sometimes they fought with each other, but she felt strong enough to cope with him.

The following year they both moved into a flat in the main street of Buffalo. She continued to find her husband Chester boring, and often went out alone in the evenings and hitched rides in cars to get to her destinations. She found being picked up exciting since she could get to know interesting men this way. She had a friend called Mary who attended wild parties with her. In the 20's in the USA when alcohol was prohibited, it was hard to come by unless you had connections in the black market. When asked about the next important event in her life, Grace described a heated dispute with her husband on the 19th April 1927, during which she injured his arm with a pair of scissors.

Next, she saw herself two weeks later with a man called Jack. He appeared to have fallen in love with her and reassured her that he wished to stay in Buffalo in order to be with her. He seemed to like everything about Grace. She now decided to leave her husband and rented a room in a hotel. In contrast to her relationship with her husband she never fought with Jack even though he showed signs of having a jealous streak. On the 17th May Chester tried to persuade her to come back to him after he had found her in the hotel. She managed to escape from him and Jack drove her to another hotel in order to rent another room. After that Jack took her to a swimming pool where she usually swam every week. Later Jack picked Ivy up from there. He had been out drinking. In the car he suggested that they should move somewhere else. Ivy told him that she would definitely want to take her son with her. He was very indignant about this. Then he got cross with her saying that the men in the pub told him that she was a whore. He also made nasty remarks about her clothes and her shoes with the red heels. The man at the reception had told him exactly whom she had slept with. She strongly contradicted him and accused him of being drunk. He called her a tart. He suddenly stopped the car, hit her, stabbed her with a knife and finally strangled her.

After death we are usually able to see everything from a *bird's perspective* without feeling any more pain. This is why Dr. Goldberg led Ivy into this state of being immediately after death. He allowed her to describe through the eyes of Grace what happened to her at that time. Jack had thrown her body into the Ellicott creek. When asked who Jack was in her present life she named her earlier friend John whom she had traded in for Dave. After this regression therapy Ivy lost her neck phobia and Dave was able to touch her neck for the first time. When asked whether Chester or her son Cliff has been reborn in her present life, she replied that they had not.

Such dramatic murder stories and other powerful occurrences from past lives are often revealed during regression therapy. I often joke with my friends about finding crime and action films rather boring after being party to so many past life regressions. Dr. Goldberg gave no great personal significance to Ivy's account, since it had been accessed in a trance state. He did not consider it his duty to double check material obtained during regression for its true content. "I don't concern myself with names, dates or places, since these have no therapeutic value." Therefore this case was added to his files. Three years later he happened to go through these notes and noticed that Ivy had used her full name, which was Grace Doze, and the place where she had lived, Buffalo, New York. She also named the day of her death as the 17th May 1927. Only now did he have the idea to write to a newspaper in Buffalo to inquire whether it existed in 1927, and whether during the third week of May there had been a news report about the murder of a woman named Mrs. Grace Doze. Neither Dr. Goldberg nor Ivy had ever been to Buffalo.

Even Dr. Goldberg was surprised by what came to light. Three Buffalo based newspapers reported in various issues about a mysterious murder, which was not solved at the time. Dr. Goldberg was then sent copies of these papers, which had been preserved on microfilm. In these papers were reports of the discovery of the body of a Mrs. Grace Doze found in the Ellicott creek. According to the medical autopsy report, knife wounds were found on her body as well as strangulation marks on her neck. She wore shoes with red heels. Daily the papers announced more details about this murder case. All of the names mentioned were accurate, except two that Ivy had talked about during hypnosis. All the details such as her surname, the husband's name, the mother's surname, the street names, the names of the hotels in which she had stayed, her visit to the swimming pool, her girlfriend's name, various incidents in her personal life, as well as the disputes with her husband were confirmed. The police had questioned her husband and held him temporarily as a possible murder suspect. Everything was completely accurate. The papers did report that Grace Doze had been 30 years old when she died, and that her son was called Chester like his father.

Dr. Goldberg told many people from television companies about this fascinating case. CBS television was the company that finally decided to make a film out of these events using famous actors. The personal history of Grace was thoroughly researched during the making of this film. From this they were able to discover her correct age, which was just as Ivy had stated and contrary to what the newspapers wrote. Another discovery was that her son was not called Chester as the papers had wrongly reported, but Clifford shortened to Cliff, just as Ivy had told us when speaking as Grace during regression. Even if Ivy had tried to deceive Dr. Goldberg by having read newspaper articles from the past and had informed herself about Grace Doze, she would have given him the wrong details. Her success during regression was only possible because she was able to spontaneously let herself go into a deep trance state. In such a trance one can no longer play roles or tell lies since what is re-lived is the actual past life experiences.

The film, Search for Grace, was broadcast by CBS on the 17th May 1994 at 11pm. Dr. Goldberg saw from the facts that it was no coincidence that this film was shown exactly 67 years to the day after the death of Grace Doze, and at the exact time of her death. He has experienced too many so-called *coincidences* to still believe that they exist. His whole outlook on life has changed through working with regression therapy. He is convinced that all the historical facts brought to light during regression can later be proven to be correct.[28]

Dear readers, what do you say now? Can you still doubt reincarnation as a fact? Even so, I do not wish to push you into a new belief, since in my opinion we gradually warm to new truths. When the time has come for a person to gain a new insight then he will be ready to accept it. My belief is that at the turn of the century there will be a radical global change in the way we think. What this could mean for our present day world I will go into in more detail at the end of this book. Now we come to some hard evidence of reincarnation which even the most critical of you will no longer be able to reject.

4

BIRTH DEFORMITIES AND BIRTHMARKS AS EVIDENCE OF REINCARNATION

IAN STEVENSON, THE COPERNICUS OF A NEW WORLD VISION

I would now like to tell you about something that is equal in importance to the discoveries of Copernicus. In the 16th Century this man unequivocally established that the earth moves around the sun, contrary to the Christian belief that the sun, the planets and the stars all rotate around the earth. This discovery had the effect of changing the whole world concept, even though the Counter Reformation tried to reverse it. This change also heralded the beginning of a new scientifically based concept of the world where only that which could be proven to be true by technical and scientific means was considered valid. Belief and intuitive knowing were no longer taken seriously.

The intellect, now the symbol of the scientific world, has driven out the belief in the beyond, in wonder, the belief in anything spiritual and even in God and godliness itself. Visions of life after death, the possibility of contact with the dead or even the return of someone in another body - namely reincarnation – didn't fit the scientific concept of the world. These are all things that were not possible to prove with technical gadgetry used as an extension of intelligence. Where there was no proof there was also no truth. The representatives of the scientific world who are still in control of the way people think in the western world at the end of the twentieth-century, see those who still believe in old or very new truths as not in their right minds. In their eyes people who believe in life after death or even reincarnation are to be pitied. They are obviously unable to think rightly and are clinging to wishful thinking or are evading the truth. This is why the so-called *evidence* in favour of reincarnation was declared false. This included evidence based on children's statements who remembered their past lives as well as evidence retrieved during regression by means of trance techniques.

Those who wave the banner of the scientific worldview are not moved in the slightest by the most convincing evidence. Whatever they are unable to prove by scientific means has no validity and is not to be taken seriously. In their view it should be either ignored or opposed. There is a whole army of such scientists who grew up with this scientific concept of the world and completely paid homage to it at the beginning of their careers. Many scientists, because of their continued interest and dedicated research into reincarnation, have come to an understanding based on the new evidence available. These new insights simply did not fit their existing concepts of life and to admit to the truth of this took great courage.

One of these brave scientists is the Canadian psychiatrist Professor Dr. Ian Stevenson, who out of curiosity, got to grips with the possibility of reincarnation in 1960. He heard of a case in Sri Lanka where a child claimed to remember a past life. After having gone there and thoroughly questioning the child's parents, the child and the people who the child claimed were its parents from the past, he was convinced that the possibility of the reality of reincarnation may be valid. He was well aware that in seeing only one case there was still the possibility of coincidence. He could only prove the rebirth of a child claiming to remember a past life scientifically, if he had evidence of many such cases that were either very similar or totally different. This would require a vast amount of work not only behind the desk where the threads of evidence would be linked and scientific reports compiled, but also by travelling all over the world wherever a case showed up. Such an undertaking would be a life's work that would involve the work of other scientific assistants as time went by. Amateur practices would not be allowed to creep into this investigation.

The more cases he pursued, the greater became his drive to scientifically solve this new territory within the many world's mysteries, which until now have been excluded from scientific observation. Nonetheless he believed he could approach it with scientific means and eventually present us with hard evidence and solutions.

In 1960 he published two articles in the Journal of the American Society for Psychical Research, about children who remembered past lives. Parapsychologists and medics open to his explanations encouraged him to continue to apply himself to this new area of research. It was only in 1974 that Dr. Stevenson published his book, Twenty cases suggestive of reincarnation. Dr. Stevenson became well known wherever this book appeared by those people who already had an interest in this subject. They were pleased to be presented with such fundamental research into reincarnation from a scientific source. When writing about various cases Stevenson is extremely careful not to jump to conclusions about the truth of reincarnation. He calls these cases which have been researched 'suggestive' of reincarnation, meaning that they have not as yet been proven. If in the past he had written about it with total conviction he could well have lost his teaching post at the University of Virginia in Charlottesville, USA. He did not want to commit himself to making such a claim as yet, because it was very clear to him that during the course of his scientific research many related questions would arise which he first hoped to follow up in greater depth. He published his research in the scientific newspapers for the scientific community to examine.

In 1987 he published his second book entitled, Children who remember past lives. Of this he says, "This book is written for the ordinary man on the street."[29] Meanwhile, the interest in reincarnation among the people had risen dramatically. Thousands of Americans attended regression seminars or one to one regressions in which they hoped to follow up their own past life experiences. The television reported many interesting cases relating to this subject. People wanted to know more about reincarnation, especially from an expert such as Stevenson who keeps himself well concealed behind his scientific image. In this book which marks a milestone in research into reincarnation he presents the reader with the most interesting cases he has researched in a simple and down-to-earth manner. He has already published some of these cases in specialist papers. This book and his articles were merely by-products of his main life's work on which he had been working for a long time, and which he hoped to complete before he died and before he will discover after death the whole truth which while living on earth is hidden from us due to our somewhat limited vision.

THE BOOK THAT WILL CHANGE OUR WAY OF THINKING

The great scientist Professor Dr. Ian Stevenson published his life's work, which was published in the autumn of 1997. It is in two volumes with a total of 2268 pages. Its title is

Reincarnation and Biology – A contribution to the Etiology of Birthmarks and Birth Defects. This monumental piece of work contains hundreds of pictures. In the first volume he mainly describes birthmarks, those distinguishing marks on the skin which the new-born baby brings into the world that cannot be put down to inheritance. In his second volume Stevenson mainly focuses on deformities and other anomalies which children are born with, which cannot be traced back to inheritance, prenatal or perinatal (created during birth) occurrences. I will give you a couple of examples from his second volume since we have been confronted with children's birthmarks on many occasions in the first part of this book.

When I encountered Professor Stevenson's extensive book for the first time in 1997 I could not put it down. I am convinced that this book will completely change our way of thinking. We will no longer view reincarnation as a hypothesis but as a reality. What this could mean for all of us I will go into in greater detail at the end of this book. Stevenson wrote his book as a scientific thesis so that the scientifically minded could study it and possibly accept it. You, dear readers, will perhaps say regretfully that this is precisely the reason that this material will not be so accessible to you. I wish to thank Dr. Stevenson for considering the 'man in the street' by publishing an easy to understand condensed version of his book, (i.e. one-tenth of his entire two-volume thesis). This he embellished with several important photographs and is called, Where

Reincarnation and Biology Intersect. This book is likely to spread like wildfire throughout America on it's way to becoming a best seller. Every critic, journalist or spiritually minded person who speaks of reincarnation will need to read this book in order to sound plausible, and be able to keep up with conversations on the subject.

During his original research into various cases involving children's memories of past lives, Stevenson enthusiastically brought to our attention the fact that these children frequently bore birthmarks which most likely related to their murder or the death they suffered in a previous life. At the time he was unaware of the fact that an in-depth study of these occurrences would be the final proof of reincarnation. The above mentioned research into birthmarks and congenital defects are more vital in establishing proof of reincarnation than children's accounts, including all the factual evidence – such as the case of Shanti Devi has shown us – for it gives us objective and illustrative evidence that fits in with the rather fragmented memories of the children and adults questioned. In many cases there are also medical documents available as further proof, which are usually compiled after the death of the person. Professor Stevenson adds that in the so called 'solved cases' he researched and in which birthmarks and deformities were present, he could see no other explanation other than that of reincarnation.[30] Only 30% - 60% of these deformities can be put down to birth defects which related to genetic factors, virus infections or chemical causes. (i.e. like those found in children damaged by the drug Contergan or alcohol). Apart from these obvious causes, the medical profession has no other explanation for the other 40% to 70% of cases than that of mere chance. Stevenson has now succeeded in giving us an explanation of why a person is born with these deformities and why they appear precisely in that part of their body and not in another.

According to Stevenson, birthmarks and congenital deformities for which no medical explanations exist can be directly linked with reincarnation. These can also be the result of how the person met his death in a previous life. There are at least five possible connections that all these cases have in common. Firstly, and the most unusual scenario, it is possible that someone who believed in reincarnation expressed a wish to be reborn to a couple or a previous partner. This is usually because they are convinced that they would be well cared for by those particular people. Such wishes are often expressed by the Tlingit Indians of Alaska and by the Tibetans. Secondly, and more frequent than this are the occurrences of prophetic dreams. Someone who has died appears to a pregnant or not as yet pregnant woman and tells her that he or she will be reborn to her. Sometimes relatives or friends have dreams like this and will then relate the dream to the mother to be. Stevenson found these prophetic dreams to be particularly prolific in Burma and among the Indians in Alaska. Thirdly, in these cultures the parents or someone experienced in this immediately check the body of a new-born child for recognisable marks to establish whether the deceased person they had once known has been reborn to them. This searching for marks of identification is very common among cultures that believe in reincarnation, and especially among the Tlingit Indians and the Igbos of Nigeria. I know that various tribes of West Africa make marks on the body of the recently deceased in order to be able to identify the person when he or she is reborn.

The most frequently occurring event relating to rebirth is a child remembering a past life. Children usually begin to talk about their memories between the ages of two and four. Such memories gradually dwindle when the child is between five and eight years old. There are of course always some exceptions, such as a child continuing to remember it's previous life but not speaking about it very often for various reasons. Most of the children talk about their previous identity with great intensity and feeling. Often they cannot decide for themselves which world is real and which one is not. They often experience a kind of double existence where at times one life is more prominent, and at times the other life takes over. This is why they usually speak of their past life in the present tense saying things like, "I have a husband and two children who live in Jaipur." Almost all of them are able to tell us about the events leading up to their death.

Children tend to talk about their previous parents rather than their present ones, and usually express a wish to return to them. When the previous family has been found and details about the person in that past life had been verified, then the fifth common denominator reveals itself. This is the noticeably unusual behaviour of the child. For instance, if the child is born in India to a very low class family and was a member of a higher caste in its previous life, it may feel uncomfortable in its new family. The child may ask to be served or waited on hand and foot and may refuse to wear cheap clothes. Stevenson gives us many examples of all these unusual behaviour patterns. In 35% of cases he investigated children who died an unnatural death developed phobias. For example, if they had drowned in a past life then they frequently developed a phobia about going out in deep water. If they had been shot, they were often afraid of guns and loud bangs. If they died in a road accident they would sometimes develop a phobia of travelling in cars, buses or lorries. Such reasons for phobias are often revealed during a regression therapy and can be swiftly dealt with and overcome. In my experience it is often the case that such phobias could become acute at exactly the time in the person's life at which the accident had occurred in their previous life. As you can see there is much work to be done in researching actual past causes that now affect present day lives. This is only the beginning, a hundred years from now many thousands of specialist books will have been written on the subject. They will give us a much clearer picture of which conditions relating to past lives trigger which phobia, at what age, of what intensity and under which conditions.

Another frequently observed unusual form of behaviour Stevenson called *Philias* concerns children who express the wish to eat different kinds of food or to wear different clothes to those of their culture. If a child had developed an alcohol, tobacco or drug addiction as an adult in a previous incarnation he may express a need for these substances and develop cravings at an early age. This confronts us with the question of whether many of today's addicts were already addicts in a previous life and are they merely continuing this habit in the present? Regression therapy could often give them relevant information and support. Many of these children with past life memories show talents that they had in their previous lives. Often children who were members of the opposite sex in their previous life show difficulty in adjusting to the new sex. These problems relating to the 'sex change' can lead to homosexuality later on in their lives. They may wish to dress as girls or prefer to play with girls rather than boys. Until now all these human oddities have been a mystery to the psychiatrists. We can no longer blame the parents for their children's behaviour. At long last research into reincarnation is shedding some light on the subject. In the past doctors blamed such peculiarities on a lack of certain hormones, now they will have to think again.

Children that died when they were adults in their previous life and are able to remember this often behave like adults in many ways. When playing with siblings or friends they automatically slot into the role of an adult. Difficulties sometimes arise if a child is reborn to a woman who used to be her daughter in a past life, for then the child usually does not want to listen to anything her previous daughter wants to tell her. Behaviour like this can of course also be found among children in general whether they remember their past lives or not.

As you can well imagine dear readers, many answers to questions are being made available to us through the extensive research into reincarnation. This work is of enormous importance to the whole of mankind. Stevenson, who acts as a representative for the scientists, is suddenly bringing many new recently discovered connections to our attention. Scientists and psychiatrists have been aware of the existence of reincarnation and regression therapy for some time now, and have been showing an interest in these issues. The fact that scientists, such as the meticulous Stevenson are showing an interest in these matters is sensational news. Stevenson came to the conclusion that in cases where children's memories of past lives and previous families cannot be explained by cryptomnesia, thought-transferral, possession or impressions received through the mother, reincarnation offers the only feasible explanation.[31]

So far we have been focusing a great deal on Prof. Stevenson, the Copernicus of our times, so now it is time to turn our attention to some cases in which reincarnation offers the only explanation. Stevenson describes these in his extensive book, Where Reincarnation and Biology Intersect. You can find the relevant illustrations to the examples I am about to present to you in his book, which will hopefully give you a more complete picture.

THE GIRL WHO WAS MURDERED WHEN SHE WAS A MAN IN HER PAST LIFE

In May 1973 a girl named Ma Hatwe Win was born in the village of Kyar-Kan not far from the town of Meiktila (pronounced Myanmar) in northern Burma. The little finger on her left hand was missing, and her left thigh and her right ankle just above the joint had indented creases all the way round. These can clearly be seen in picture 29 of the book. Similar indentations were found at the base of the fingers of her left hand. There were also birthmarks on her chest just above her heart and on her head.

When her mother was three months pregnant she had a terrible dream. She dreamt a man crawling on all fours, whose legs appeared to have been amputated from the knees down, was following her. He followed her into her house. She ran outside but he continued to follow her, even though she begged him not to. She woke up, but when she finally got back to sleep she again dreamt of the man with the amputated legs following her, and woke up very frightened.

When Ma Htwe Win was two years old she showed her grandfather her legs saying, "Look how cruel they have been to me Grandad." When he asked her who had been so cruel to her, she told him that this had happened when she had been a man called Nga Than. She said that three men called Than Doke, Nga Maung and Chan Paw had killed her. When the girl's parents returned from the fields the grandfather told them about what their daughter had said. As time went by the girl was able to recall more and more details about her own previous death. She told her parents that she remembers being a man, and standing face to face with three men wielding sabres. He had defended himself as well as he could until his sabre had become stuck in a wall. Then the attackers had stabbed him, chopped off several of his fingers and hit him over the head.

Lying on the ground his attackers must have taken him for dead, but he could still hear them discussing how they could best hide his body.[32] They decided to make his body as small as possible so as to fit it into a medium-sized sack. His legs had been bent up behind his back and his ankles tied together with rope. They put him in the sack and threw him into a dried up well.

Another time the girl told her parents that Nga Than's wife had had an affair with his friend Than Doke, which was why the two men had fallen out with each other. Nga Than had owned a grocer's shop and Than Doke was one of three business partners who had been his murderers. It was later discovered that Nga Than's wife had wanted to be free of her husband and had hired the three men to murder him. When she had been questioned about the disappearance of her husband, she had told the police that he had moved south. This kind of separation was a common occurrence so they suspected no foul play. The deserted wife now married Than Doke.

One day when he was drunk he had an argument with his
wife, and was over heard telling her exactly how he had killed
her previous husband and where the body had been hidden.
The police were informed and on searching the dried up well
found the body. Both the woman and the men responsible
for the murder were arrested, but were later released due to
lack of evidence.

What is interesting is that a pregnant woman was passing
the well as the police were retrieving the murdered victim's
body. It was during the night after this experience that the
woman had the dreams about the man following her. She
had perceived him with parts of his legs missing because
they had been tied up behind his back. Ma Htwe Win
remembered watching her body being pulled out of the well
while hovering over the scene as a spirit being still connected
to the earth. She had then seen the pregnant woman among
the crowd of inquisitive onlookers and had chosen her as
her future mother.

Apparently Ma Htwe Win parents' had not let on to anyone
who their daughter really was. One-day, at their daughter's
request, they took her to the cafe run by the wife of the
murdered man. When a boy not much older than Ma Htwe
Win came into the café, she immediately recognised him as
her son. (Do you remember Shanti Devi's meeting with her
son?) This boy asked his mother for some money. Before
she had the chance to give it to him, Ma Htwe Win had

already asked her own mother for some money and had given it to the boy. After this the two children had held hands and cried. Suddenly the girl begged her parents to leave the café as quickly as possible because Doke was coming. Once outside her father asked her who Doke was. The girl told him that he was the man who had murdered her.

Ma Htwe Win felt more drawn to boys than girls and preferred wearing boys' clothes, but her mother soon put a stop to this. Even so, when Stevenson went to visit her in order to find out more details, she sat opposite him wearing shorts, which was seen as improper for girls in Burma. She was embarrassed about her legs and vowed to take revenge of her murderers one day. When Stevenson suggested that it wasn't very lady like to carry out this threat, she said that nonetheless she intended to find a way of revenging herself. The deformed part of her legs matched the areas on the corpse where the man's legs had been tightly bound with rope. The left little finger was also missing on both the girl and the murder victim.[33] After reading about this case, can anyone still doubt this evidence for reincarnation? We shall move onto the next case.

LOST A LEG IN A TRAIN ACCIDENT — LATER REBORN WITHOUT A LEG

Tatkon is a fairly small town in Burma (Myanmar) which is situated directly on the main Rangoon (Yangon) to Mandalay railway line. Most of the trains stop at this station and many locals, most of them women and children, use this opportunity to sell water, fruit, various foods and other things to the passengers through the open windows. They usually stand on the platform or on the central rail track. Two women Daw Than Kyi and the slightly younger Daw Ngwe Kyi were good friends. Both of them sold water to the passengers. The former woman had a sixteen-year-old daughter who on August 19th 1966 was selling red roses from the central track, which ran between the two lines bordering the platforms. This girl was called Ma Thein New, and due to her dark skin colour she had given herself the nickname Kalamagyi. Her mother was also there working from one of the platforms.

On that particular day the points man was unable to shift the rails for the oncoming train because they had become jammed, so the train continued along the central rail instead of running along the track alongside the platform as usual. Kalamagyi was standing on the central track oblivious to any danger, since she knew from experience that the incoming train would switch to the other track on its way in. The man operating the points saw her and shouted at her to get off the track, but it was too late and the train hit her. When the train stopped, the lower part of her right leg was found several metres away from the rest of her body, which had to be retrieved in parts from under the wheels. Her parents later buried the pieces in the family grave.

Shortly after this a friend of Kalamagyi's mother had a dream in which she saw Kalamagyi standing before her completely healed saying, "I will come back to be with you." In the dream the woman answered, "How could you come to me? You were run down by a train!" Not long after she again dreamt of Kalamagyi who now begged to be granted the wish to be reborn as her daughter. Finally the woman agreed and told several neighbours about the dreams, which had occurred about two months before she became pregnant. Kalamagyi also appeared to her former mother in a dream and told her that she owed a certain woman some money. Another woman whom she mentioned in the dream also owed Kalamagyi money that her mother was to ask for. When she went to the woman to discuss this outstanding debt, the woman said that Kalamagyi had already appeared to her to remind her of this.

On July 26th 1967 Mrs. Daw Ngwe Kyi gave birth to a girl who was given the name Ma Khin Mar Htoo. The lower part of her right leg was missing. (See picture 25 in the relevant book). Her hands too had deformities, her left thumb was a mere stump. The mother knew immediately that this girl was Kalamagyi who had appeared in the dream asking to be reborn as her daughter. Even in her early years she began to call herself Kalamagyi. When she was three she told her uncle that this was her name and that a train at the station had killed her. She also told a relative the name of her previous father. One of her aunts wanted to test just how much she would remember of her previous life by reminding her of the roses she had given her to sell from Kalamagyi's mother's field on the day of the accident. The little girl then corrected her telling her where the roses had really come from. This was correct as her aunt then confirmed. When the three-year-old accompanied her mother to the train station, she saw her previous mother among the saleswomen and called out to her, "Mother!"

This woman then took the little girl, who hopped on one leg or crawled on all fours, home and showed her some family photographs. The little girl called each person portrayed by name, even using nicknames that she had given them when she was Kalamagyi. At another meeting she recognised her uncle and a brother from her past. She addressed them both with their correct names. Since both families knew each other and her old family totally accepted her as the fatally injured Kalamagyi, she spent much time with them. Her two houses were only 350 metres apart. When she was about four years old she expressed a wish to go and visit her father from her past life who now lived in a different part of the town. When she was taken there she immediately recognised him and wanted to hug him and sit on his lap.

As time went by, the one legged girl could even recall what it had been like after her death. Apparently she had been trapped at the scene of her accident for some time, but had also been witness to her body parts being buried at her funeral. She insisted that one of her legs had not been accounted for. The truth of this matter could not be proven. When asked at which point in time she had decided to be born to her present mother, she answered, "I already knew her very well and had often watched her selling water, and one day I followed her home."

Ma Khin Mar Htoo had a great fear of trains as a child, even just going near railway lines frightened her. Another peculiarity she had in common with Kalamagyi was that she refused to eat pork.

When Stevenson visited the thirteen-year-old in 1980, she was walking on crutches. She confided in him that she still had the wish to live with her past family. When asked how she explains the fact of her deformities and her left thumb missing she replied, "I lost these a long time ago when the wheels of a train rolled over me." Her memories of being Kalamagyi were still relatively clear. When Stevenson again visited her four years later she only had vague memories of her former life. Meanwhile she had been fitted with an artificial limb that enabled her to move around freely.[34]

Is it not strange how such impaired limbs or even limb amputations can imprint themselves on the body of a person when reborn? What as yet undiscovered laws are behind all this? Who or what decides why a reincarnated person must return to this world with such *marks of recognition*, whilst another person, after having died a gruesome death with the loss of limbs is born with a perfect body? Are these laws also governed by karma? We are not aware of the true reasons as yet, but we are beginning to collect evidence and to carry out comparisons. Theories will no doubt follow these discoveries and facts, and one-day we will discover the law that governs the fate of those who return to earth with birthmarks or deformities. Let us now turn our attention to another most informative case which Stevenson's colleague Resat Bayer investigated in 1966. Stevenson himself went to Turkey a year later in order to further research this case.

SHOT ACCIDENTALLY BY HIS NEIGHBOUR

On May 9th 1958 Selim Fesli, a 47 years old Turk, had been working in his field bordering his neighbour's vineyard. His neighbour was called Isa Dirbekli. In the early evening Selim frequently rode home to his village Hatun Koy on his donkey. Imagine how surprised his family were when the donkey arrived home without his master on its back. Something was wrong. They hurried to where he had been working and found Selim on the ground. He was in pain and his face was covered in blood from a gunshot wound. He was still breathing and able to react to them, but could not speak. They tried to get him to say who had shot him but he could utter no name. He seemed to indicate that it was someone from the village. The police only arrived at the scene of the crime hours later, and then finally a taxi took him to the hospital in

the neighbouring village of Iskenderum in southeast Turkey.
He died six days later. He had been unable to give them
the name of his murderer.

The police arrested two suspects, one of which was his
neighbour Isa Dirbekli. He admitted to having accidentally
shot his friend while out hunting with his shotgun. He had
seen something moving in the grass, thought it was a rabbit
and had pulled the trigger. When he heard screams he had
hurried over to see what had happened. Selim had been lying
on the ground taking a nap when Isa shot him in the ear.
There was blood flowing from his ear and parts of his face.
Isa Dirbekli had panicked and left the scene of the crime
as fast as he could. When asked why he had not helped Selim
or at least called for help he said that he had been afraid of
the revenge of Selim's sons. The judges later accepted the
fact that it had been a sad accident and found Isa's story
so believable that he was only sentenced to two years in
prison. The victim's sons also seemed to see their father's
death as an unfortunate accident, and therefore backed away
from taking any revengeful action. Even so, Selim's father
was convinced that this shooting had been no accident. Even
though Isa was his friend and neighbour he knew that his
son had been in conflict with him at that time. The autopsy
report, which was handed to Dr. Stevenson in order to give
him greater insight into this case, stated that six holes were
found in the area of the right side of his face and right ear.
After opening the skull they determined that shotgun pellets
had entered his brain.

Two kilometres from Hatun Koy is the village of Sarkonak. It was there in 1958 that Mrs. Karanfil Tutusmus was in her late pregnancy awaiting the birth of her second child. Two days before the birth of her son, whose name was to be Semih, she had a dream. In this dream she saw a man enter her room. She asked him why he had come and told him to leave since her husband was presently in Ankara. He told her that his name was Selim Fesli and that he had been shot in the ear. When Mrs. Tutusmus awoke she remembered that a man with this name from the neighbouring village had recently been accidentally killed. When her husband returned she told him about this dream. Her husband Ali Tutusmus, the owner of a vegetable stall, had known the recently deceased man very well and could accurately describe him to her.

Semih was born with a right ear that was small and deformed, (see picture 28 in the book). At the early age of one and a half he did not want to be called Semih, insisting that his real name was Selim. He even used his old surname, Fesli, which was exactly the name the man had used in Mrs. Tutusmus' dream shortly before Semih's birth. As time went by Semih revealed to his mother that Isa Dirbekli had murdered him, intentionally shooting him in the ear. At the age of four he walked the two kilometres to the neighbouring village of Hatun Koy on his own and went into his former wife's house and told her, "I am Selim, you are my wife Katibe." He could describe many incidents in great detail from their former lives together. Semih saw a basket woven out of reeds and said, "I bought you this basket, and you still keep it where I first put it."This comment convinced Mrs. Katibe that he really was her deceased husband Selim. Later he saw his daughter and sons from his past and called them by their correct names.

From then on Semih often went to Hatun Koy alone, even though he had been forbidden to do so and often got beaten for it. He could not resist the urge to return to his previous home and village and to his former family who welcomed him with open arms. One day he met a man who had heard that he apparently was the deceased Selim and asked him, "Do you know who I am?" The little chap answered immediately, "I know you very well. You are Ali Battihi." He had been Selim's former neighbour.

Sometimes he would go to Hatun Koy five or six times a week. It made no difference to him that his children from his previous life were all much older than he was; he treated them as if he was their father often meddling in their family affairs. Since they all seemed convinced that he was their deceased father they let him be. When Taju, Selim's second son got married, Semih had not been invited to the wedding. He felt so insulted that he stopped visiting his former family for two months. In order to rectify this mistake, he was invited to the engagement party of Hassan, Selim's youngest son. Semih asked his father for some money to give to his *son* for his engagement. His father had long accepted the fact that his son also belonged to another family and gave him the money. When Hassan was married a year later, Semih's father gave him an even larger sum of money for the bridegroom.

When Semih was eight years old Mrs. Katibe Fesli wanted to remarry. When Semih heard of this, he went straight to Hatun Koy to have a talk with the man who was trying to win his wife, and threatened to kill him if he tried to marry her. To Katibe he said reproachfully, "How dare you attempt to marry another man as well as me!" Katibe then told the boy that she had no intention of remarrying. Three years later Katibe died. When Semih heard of this he went straight to Hatun Koy. The twelve-year-old boy was so shaken by this that he arrived in tears. Neighbours later commented on the fact that Semih seemed to mourn the death of Katibe more than her own sons did. An aunt later found Semih at Katibe's grave where he sat and cried for a long time. She also claimed to have seen him lying unconscious by the grave one day, and in order to bring him around had poured a bucket of water over him.

Isa Dirbekli turned his hand to a new profession after being released from prison. He now sold Raki-Schnapps, which he carried around with him in bottles. When the eight-year-old Semih saw Isa he picked up some stones and threw them at him, smashing one of his bottles. Whenever he saw Isa after that he always picked up stones and threw them at the street trader, saying that one-day when he was grown up he would seek revenge. Semih had not forgotten the events from the past. He had been in conflict with his friend and neighbour Isa about occasionally letting his donkey stray into his vineyard. While Selim was lying down for a short nap, Isa had once again found the donkey in his vineyard. He had grabbed his gun and in anger had fired a round at the sleeping man. Then he had opened the man's bleeding mouth and spat into it. In his superstitious beliefs this meant that the dead or injured person could no longer give away any information about his aggressor, and as we know, this is what happened. Stevenson later met up with Isa and asked him about the truth of Selim's death. He denied having killed him intentionally and finally admitted that he feared Semih's revenge.

At the age of eighteen when Semih was doing his military service he was given an artificial ear, which at first glance was not recognisable as such. Stevenson's Turkish partner, Resat Bayer, took it upon himself to attempt to free Semih of his feelings of revenge by presenting him with this likely scenario: if he was to kill Isa, Isa could be reborn and then likewise take revenge on him. This scenario could then continue indefinitely from one life to the next. Having seen the likelihood of this Semih changed his attitude towards his murderer, even though as he later admitted he still felt the urge to throw stones every time he saw him.[35]

Stevenson presents us with many similar examples in his extensive book. He reports on those reborn with birthmarks or birth deformities relating to past lives, and on those remembering their previous lives at an early age. Some of these children remember the circumstances in past lives, which led to the scars or the loss of certain limbs in their present life. These examples are clearly illustrated with various photographs. Now I wish to tell you of the latest discoveries about reincarnation, which are surprisingly new, even to me. In the following chapter I will present you with evidence of so-called albinos, white skinned people born to dark skinned races, who in many cases can trace their skin colour to having been white in a past life and are now reincarnated in dark skin cultures.

SHOT DOWN OVER BURMA AS AN AMERICAN DURING THE WAR—LATER REBORN IN THE SAME PLACE

During World War two, Burma renamed Myanmar, was occupied by the Japanese. At the end of the war the British with the help of the American air force, which was based in India at that time, forced their Japanese opponents to retreat. Many British and Japanese lost their lives in this conflict, and several American planes were shot down. In the following years several white skinned children were born among the Burmese people. This was years after any white skinned people had been resident in this country. Many of these albino children began to talk about being English or Japanese at a very young age and claimed to have died in the war. They found it rather difficult to adjust to their new culture. They refused to eat the spicy food that the Burmese are very fond of, and asked to use spoons and forks to avoid eating with their hands. They preferred to wear white people's clothes and shoes and refused to wear the traditional lungyi, (an ankle long cloth tied around the waist). They wanted to play with European toys and often called themselves by their names from a past life. Some asked to be allowed to go home. Among these white skinned albinos Stevenson found an American co-pilot who claimed to have been reborn after being shot down over Burma during the war.

Approximately 120km south of the Burmese town of Mandalay lies the provincial town of Meiktila. On the 9th May 1950 Mrs. Daw Kjin Htwe gave birth to her first child. Her husband U Tin Aung was a teacher and later the director of a public school. His wife was shocked when she saw that her child had white skin and facial features similar to those of European children. What would people say? Thank God there were no white Europeans in their town since the British pulled out two years ago, otherwise people might have suspected her of having been unfaithful to her husband. This fear was to be put to rest as time went by, since out of her 11 children that followed, three more were born white skinned. In both her husband's and her own family there had never been any albinos, which meant that this phenomenon could not be genetic. The child was given the name Maung Zaw Win Aung. (Please see picture 34 in the relevant book).

The boy was brought up by his parents and two aunts. At the age of three the little boy Zaw talked about being called John Steven and spoke about having been an American air man who was shot down. Soon he was making even more detailed claims. He said that he had not been the pilot but the pilot's friend and that he used to drink alcohol before going into action. The Japanese had shot their plane down near Meiktila. When he overheard people talking about the bombs that were dropped on their town in 1945, the three-year-old would say, "Why would you have been afraid? It was me who was flying over the town." Zaw had mixed feelings about aeroplanes. On the one hand he was fascinated by them and was drawing them at an early age, but on the other hand he was terrified of them. If an aeroplane flew overhead while he was playing with his friends he would panic and shout, "Hide!" or "Get down!" One day, at his request, his parents took him to an airport. They talked to several pilots about Zaw claiming to have been an American airman in his previous life. When one of the pilots heard about this he said that he would happily take him on a flight one day. The three-year old answered, "I don't want to because when you fly in planes you get shot down."

When he was given a tricycle he suddenly rode off saying, "Come with me, I'm off to America." He had often made such statements to his aunt about going to America, who then tried to suppress his longing by feeding him duck eggs. This, according to the beliefs of their region, is the most effective cure for helping children forget their past lives.

This *cure* had no effect on the boy.

At times he would brag about having been a great airman, and at other times he seemed to regret having killed people with the bombs he dropped. This gave him no peace. At the age of 4 he started going to Buddhist monks, asking them to grant him absolution. One of them explained to him that the reason he was born in Burma and not in America was for karmic reasons. He was here to put things right by acknowledging his sins. Following this, his boastful attitude towards having been a great fighter changed. Even so at the age of 16 he still wanted to be a pilot, but his parents managed to talk him out of it.

When he was a small boy he once saw a tray with a picture of an American house and church on it. He said it reminded him of home. He still had romantic ideas about America and often expressed the wish to fly there one day.

As a child Zaw wanted to wear shoes even though all the other children went barefoot or wore sandals. He also demanded to have a uniform just like the one he had worn in his past. He managed to persuade his parents to allow him to wear trousers instead of the traditional lungyi, which all the other children and many of the adults wore. Zaw also had a dislike of the hot spicy food of his country. He loved to drink soft drinks or milk, was very fond of eating biscuits and insisted on eating with a spoon instead of using his fingers like everyone else. Zaw also seemed to crave alcohol. (You may recall that he was drunk at the time he was shot down. The circumstances in which we died can continue to affect us in our present life.) Ever since he was a child he hated the Japanese for having shot him down. There was a young boy in the neighbourhood who claimed to have been a Japanese soldier in the past. Whenever he saw Zaw he would panic and scream. Could it be that he had died because of the bombs John Stevens had dropped, or possibly at the hands of some Europeans or Americans?

There is so much us humans are not fully aware of as yet. It seems to me that we know very little about what really surrounds us and about the laws that govern our lives. I find it exciting to gradually unravel more and more of life's mysteries. Stevenson is one of those people who succeeded in doing just that.

Zaw's story is not yet finished. When he was a child he was looking at an English book and suddenly said regretfully, "I used to be able to read this." When he went to school, he was extremely good at English. He was given awards for his essays, which were printed and sent to other schools as examples. The teachers were amazed at his knowledge of the English language. (I know from my work with regression therapy that we often resist learning languages that we spoke while living in a certain country in the past in which we had an unpleasant experience or a terrifying death. On the other hand we seem to find it easy to learn a language we spoke in a life which was joyful. Our preferences for or against certain languages are governed by our past experiences; no matter at what time these may have occurred.) Zaw later became a successful doctor.

When Zaw was 10 years old his mother had a dream. In this dream a white woman aged about 25 wearing European clothing appeared to her asking to be reborn as her child. Mrs. Daw Kyin Htwe replied, "Please don't come to us, we are very poor." The woman then told her, "I don't mind that as long as I can be with my brother again." On the 21st April 1961 Mrs. Daw Kyin Htwe gave birth to an albino daughter, who not only had pale skin but also Caucasian features. When their friends saw her they commented on the fact that she looked like an English doll. This is why her parents named her Dolly. This girl had expressed nothing that could possibly be related to a past life, yet she exhibited many traits that were not part of the Burmese culture. She insisted on eating with a spoon, and if refused it she would scream. She often talked to herself in a language no one could understand. Her father thought it must be English. She developed a very close friendship with her brother Zaw that was rather unusual. At night she chose to lie down next to him on his bed and often talked to him in her strange language. When going for walks she always held Zaw's hand, which is seen as unusual among the Burmese. One day when she was asked to leave her aunt's house while Zaw was to remain there, she insisted on him coming with her, or her staying with him. She cried terribly when she was forced to leave him. She also kissed her parents on the mouth, which was most unusual in Burma. For years she refused to eat rice, but asked to have bread, butter and milk instead. Just like her brother she too wanted to wear Western clothes.

Dolly told her brother that someone else looking like them was going to be born into their family. And so it was. On the 19th October 1969 the third albino child was born. After the mother had given birth to 11 children her husband decided that she should be sterilised. Shortly before this operation was due she had a dream. A young man with blond hair came riding towards her on an elephant saying, "Please don't allow yourself to be sterilised now. I also want to come to you. I am one of your family." In November 1974 Mrs. Daw Kyin Htwe gave birth to her third albino child.

Stevenson visited the woman regularly. One day he asked her how she copes with having three albino children. She told him that it makes no difference to her and that before Zaw's birth she had never wished for albino children.

Of course Stevenson checked whether a man named John Steven had really existed and been shot down over Burma in 1945. He could not determine whether the names John Steven were both Christian names, and to which unit the soldier had belonged. These details would first have to be clarified in order to find his name in the lists of soldiers who had died in the war. [36]

Since Zaw speaks good English I am tempted to go and look

him up one day, to lead him into his past life. This would prove whether or not his life in America and all the dates relating to his life as a soldier were indeed correct. For then we would have double proof of his past life in America. I find it very tempting to research a case like this, where we are dealing with children's memories of past lives having used trance induced regression techniques. During trance things are often revealed which would normally not surface during spontaneous flashes of past memories. I can imagine that in the future we will work together more closely with others on this subject.

Even without double proof such as this one, the cases portrayed and substantiated by photographic evidence by Professor Stevenson in his thesis are enough evidence to state with certainty that reincarnation is no longer a debatable subject. The knowledge that many cultures have long possessed and the wise people of this earth have spoken about has now become common knowledge. This foundation is now so solid it can no longer be shaken. We have to thank Professor Ian Stevenson for the actual breakthrough leading to the acceptance of reincarnation. His pioneering achievements will one day rank among those of Freud and Einstein.

I think you will agree with me that anyone who has read this evidence and is still not convinced of reincarnation can not be taken seriously. He must be either stuck in his old ways of thinking, or is evading the truth because he is not ready to incorporate new concepts into his belief system. Maybe he is caught up in wishful thinking that forbids him to believe in repeated lives on earth. The most likely reason for this would be that he himself does not wish to be reborn. I will now share some thoughts on how our views on life may change when we accept reincarnation as a fact.

5

THE MEANING OF REINCARNATION IN RELATION TO A NEW CONCIOUSNESS

HOW THE CONCEPT OF REINCARNATION MAY INFLUENCE YOUR PERSONAL LIFE

1. I am no longer afraid of death, since I know that I have almost definitely lived before and am likely to reincarnate on earth again after an *in-between life* in a less dense reality.

2. When someone close to me dies it is natural to be sad. But my sadness is much reduced by knowing that he (or she) has not died but continues to live on another plane of existence. I know that he is likely to be with me often, even if I cannot see him. I also know that it was right for him to die at that time according to his fate, which was decided by a higher consciousness. I also feel that I will see this

person again after my death or in a following life on earth. Good byes forever do not exist.

3. I am tolerant towards all people as long as they do not restrict my freedom and that of others. I tolerate any form of religious practices and other people's opinions as long as they give others the same right to express themselves freely. We humans develop by broadening our awareness from one life to the next. I am never arrogant in my response towards other people's ways of thinking. I may have been that way in a previous life, and for that reason I never push my convictions onto others. Every human being reaches his time for broadening his consciousness when it is right for him. Besides, it is clear to me that it is most likely that I will often change, i.e. broaden my outlook in my future lives.

4. I will never discriminate against other people no matter who they may be. I know that it is futile for me to discriminate against someone of the opposite sex since I most likely belonged to that sex at some time myself. I will not condemn someone with a different skin colour or of a different nationality or race, since I could easily have been of this colour or race at some point in time, or possibly will be in the future. If I discriminate against someone on the grounds of being part of a different race I will then have to experience being part of that race in order to broaden my understanding and love for them. I will never look down on other people because they are poor, disabled, unattractive

or in some way different, since every person has chosen precisely their circumstances, looks, and their particular disposition in order to learn from it.

5. I will never envy others, be they richer, more powerful, cleverer, healthier or physically more beautiful, since they have created this learning situation for themselves in their life. They can use these means at their disposal to learn whatever they can in order to grow spiritually. I could possibly have had the same means at my disposal in a previous life or will have in a future incarnation. It seems necessary for us to experience all learning possibilities in order to evolve spiritually.

6. If I have a child I will give him the chance to develop his talents as long as they are not destructive. I will not force my will on him or attempt to break his, since I know that this child's past lives have played a major part in forming his present life. He will want to live out his learning programme in this life, which may be completely different to my own. This is why I will respect his individuality. Apart from all this I know that he has been an adult in a past life, possibly even one of my deceased relatives or friends. I would watch carefully whether he mentions anything about his past lives. I will not forbid him these expressions or dismiss them as crazy talk. Perhaps this child has been my partner, mother, father or friend in a past life. I also know that it is possible that I could be reborn to my present child in a future life.

7. I know that I did not choose my partner by accident. I already knew her or him from an earlier life. We decided during our life after death to return to earth to continue learning from each other. Each partnership is a learning situation in the school of life. I wish to make the most of all situations from which I can learn something.

8. I am able to accept my parents just how they are, since I freely chose them before my birth. They provided me with precisely those conditions that I need to accomplish my specific tasks in this life.

9. I see people, events and twists of fate which come my way as important pointers, which enable me to learn exactly that which is of importance to me. I allow no envy to develop in me towards others, since they most likely have very different issues to deal with and different means at their disposal for dealing with them. This is why I calmly face my specific life conditions seeing them more as learning opportunities than anything else. I do not complain about them but ask myself what it is I could learn from each situation.

10. The earth is a school of learning. With each incarnation we learn to be more understanding, more tolerant and above all more loving. If after many incarnations we have become totally loving, then we are free to leave this earthly school having passed our examinations. We will then be allowed to move on to higher universities, where we are taught greater wisdom and deeper Love.

11. I know that whenever I resist love I myself will one day be the one who is treated without love. It is only through this that I learn to be more loving with my thoughts, words and deeds. Everything I do to hurt others will one day hurt me. The laws of karma that govern this learning process are always just. Unfairness does not exist for me. This is why I don't put blame onto other people or situations; instead I ask myself what it is I need to learn from a situation in order to balance things out from an earlier life. Nothing happens by chance.

12. I know that everything in life has a purpose. Nothing is senseless. Everything that comes my way has some kind of meaning for me. This is why I will endeavour to find the purpose behind everything that happens to me.

13. I know that it is entirely upto to me how quickly I evolve spiritually. I myself am responsible for whatever happens to me, since both these things are born out of the thoughts I held, words I spoke or deeds I acted out in my past lives. In order to live another life on earth in joy and love I will use my present life to give others much joy and love. I am the creator of my own luck. I can hold no one else responsible since I am, was and will be responsible for everything that happens to me whatever that may be.

14. I see life as a gift, in which each life on earth is an opportunity to develop myself more and more in love and understanding. It pleases me to help others in their development and to allow them to help me on my journey.

Therefore I am grateful for each day I am given to learn and discover more about love. I am grateful to be given the chance to turn my consciousness more and more towards the laws of life and God's love.

HOW THE CONCEPT OF REINCARNATION MAY INFLUENCE SOCIETY AS A WHOLE

1.   Knowledge of reincarnation is beneficial. We will see every person having equal rights and there will be no more discrimination. Intentional dishonesty or victimisation, even when following orders, will be seen to create personal karma

2.   The laws of karma will become a commonly known fact, which states: what you consciously do to another you will one-day experience yourself, either in this life or another. The law of Karma is always just. Every atrocity carries a karmic debt. The law of Karma serves the learning process.

3.   When everyone knows that it is possible to have lived in any country or with any race, or members of a certain religion, or could do so at some time in the future, we develop a sense of belonging together. When this occurs there will be no more competitive thinking between the different states of this world, no more working against each other, but rather with each other. It will be a one-world

community in which we will treat every other human being with care, tolerance and understanding.

4.   In emergency situations we will be more willing to help each other, knowing that among the people of some distant part of this planet who are suffering starvation or some other major catastrophe there may be among them some of our relatives and friends from a past life. If particular nations ignore the needs of others this will again create karma for them. Therefore we will be able to offer our help more readily to those in need. There will be a general increase in the involvement of other people's well-being wherever they live in this world.

5.   Everyone will develop a totally different awareness of belonging and will accept responsibility as being part of the state. If for instance, I deceive the state by withholding taxes, something will one day be taken from me for karmic reasons. What I do to the state or to another individual one day will be done to me. This is why honesty is the best insurance policy for your future life.

6.   Before man becomes a globally responsible citizen he will feel the need to share all the responsibilities as a citizen of his particular state. If he continues to live just for his own interests and is using in an unfair manner the state to his benefit he will one day find himself in situations where he is used. Egocentric thinking and actions are a guarantee for experiencing unfairness and lovelessness in a later life.

7. Religious sects and world religions will integrate reincarnation into their belief systems in order to have a chance of survival when this knowledge becomes widely accepted. There is no such thing as a single life, only a cycle of single lives. With every life the soul becomes more complete. Reincarnation is the most just religion, giving everyone the chance when once again incarnated on earth, to rectify that which he resisted; namely loving his fellow man. God is no longer the bad guy who allows crippled babies to be born or millions of people to starve to death or die in wars.

8. Regression therapy will have a large role to play in the future. In society, drug addicts and alcoholics will be led back to the cause of their addiction in order to delete the programming that caused their addiction in the first place. Psychiatry will no longer be imaginable without regression therapy. For instance, an unusual urge to harm oneself or others may have its origins in a past life; which in the first place have to be uncovered and then cleared through regression therapy. The National Health Service will pay for training regression therapists and will happily take on board the cost of this therapy. This will save on other extremely high costs for existing therapies that are usually slow to work. Regression therapy can prove being successful in a very short space of time.

9. In the field of psychology many old and much loved theories will need to be replaced with new ones in order to

make more space for reincarnation. Universities will found new courses in psychology based on reincarnation.

10.   The medical profession will have to do much rethinking. Through the discoveries made by Professor Stevenson, MD, we now know that birth deformities may not be genetic or caused by viruses, but in most cases can be traced back to previous lives, and in particular in past causes of death. Reincarnation will also play a large part in surgery. In many cases, before conducting an operation that is not entirely necessary the doctor or surgeon will refer the patient to a regression therapist. Here will be decided, for example in the case of a vagatomy, whether or not a wound received in a previous life had already weakened the stomach area. If this is the case then it is advisable to treat it with regression therapy. Failing this, symptoms of some kind or other are likely to continue to manifest in that area. For example, if a person was killed in a previous life by a spear wound to the kidney area, he will often experience chronic pain in this region, even if doctors cannot find anything wrong with him. The co-operation between the medical profession and the regression therapists will become an obvious necessity.

11.   Once we know that we will almost definitely be reborn on this earth, keeping the planet clean and healthy will become an obvious thing to do. This will enable us to return to a healthy planet where we will be able to continue our spiritual journey. We will care more about our surroundings and will not allow the earth to become polluted.

12.   Philosophy will praise those great philosophers who are already advocating this knowledge of reincarnation. The acceptance of reincarnation creates a whole new way of thinking, and will create new philosophical schools of thought, which will not rely on abstract thinking. Instead they will be built on the integrated knowledge uncovered through regressions into past lives. The *after life* will also be thoroughly investigated. This is where we exist as souls before being reincarnated on earth. Philosophy will pose amongst many the question: Who or what created this system of reincarnation and the afterlife, for what reason and why? Ontology will gain a completely new perspective as we endeavour to get in touch with the basic truth of creation itself through trance exprinces or possibly through spiritual insights.

13.   The arts will gain tremendous momentum, since a new creative theme will be opened up to them in which public demand could become huge for anything related to the theme of reincarnation. Film, television, theatre and especially literature will no doubt adopt this theme. The representations of people and their motives for certain behaviour will be reflected against a background of their past lives in which the laws of karma will play an important part.

14.   We will concern ourselves less with reputation, power or ownership, since we will know that it is more important to nurture the love inside ourselves. This is why we will be more inclined to collect inner riches instead of outer ones. We will treat life with more respect and will view being able

to spend time on this earth as a valuable gift, the opportunity to learn more and more about love and Gods' laws. Reincarnation will contribute immensely towards making this world more beautiful and loving and one in which it is a blessing to be allowed to live, love and learn.[37]

REFERENCES

1. See Matthaeus pp 7-15, 17, 10-13, Markus 9, 11-13.

2. I got this information from an acquaintance who discussed it with the Pope. According to him approximately 80 Cardinals (out of over 130) are still resisting the acceptance of Reincarnation.

3. This report can be found in Tag Powell's book *ESP for Children* p 151+

4. In his book *Reincarnation and Biology* p 2045 Stevenson claims that the woman had not been drunk or debilitated by drugs, but had recently lost a court case in which she lost the right to care for her children. Apparently she ran the three children down because she was so angry about this situation. She was later admitted to a psychiatric ward.

5. This story is retold by Jan Wilson op.cit., p 15+ and can also be found in Stevenson's book *Reincarnation and Biology*, p 2041+

6. In my report about Shanti Devi I mainly followed Jeffry Iverson's description from his book p 168+. This journalist went to India in the late 80s and was able to interview people who had witnessed the events at that time; e.g. Shanti Devi's father. I took some of the details from the book *I have lived before* by Sture Lönnerstrand. The author had visited India in the 50s. Apart from many accounts from the witnesses he also had the committee reports at his disposal, which had been investigated at the time. This book has probably got the most detailed description of Shanti Devi's case. This case is one of the most thoroughly and successfully researched cases in favour of reincarnation, which can be traced back to a child's memories.

7. This account can be followed up in Stevenson's book *Twenty Cases of Reincarnation*, on p 200+.

8. .The account of Corliss Chotkin jun. Can be found in Stevenson's book *Twenty Cases of Reincarnation*

9. These statements can be found on p 246 in the book *Claims of Reincarnation*.

10. This account can be found in Brad Steiger's book *You will live again*, p 151+

11. A detailed description of this case can be read in Jeffrey Iverson's book *In search of the dead*, p 187+

12. The case of Titu also appeared in German newspapers in the nineties. You can read about it in paper *Esotera*, Oct. 1993 issue or in the German *Bild Zeitung*/spring 1990.

13. In the book *Lifetimes- True accounts of reincarnation,* you will find many true stories, condensed by Dr. Frederick Lenz. The story you have been reading can be found on p 22+.

14. This chapter can be found in Yonassan Gershom's book *From Ashes to Healing,* p 12+.

15. An account of this story can be found in Brad Steiger's book *You will Live Again,* p 141+

16. Frederick Lenz op. cit., p 25+.

17. Brad Steiger's book *You will Live Again,* p 178+.

18. Frederick Lenz op. cit., p 26+.

19. My account is mainly based on her book *Across Time and Death,* and also on her condensed version *Meeting her past-life Children,* which is mentioned in Sue Carpenter's book *Past Lives-True stories of Reincarnation,* p 211+.

20. Dick Sutphen op. cit., p 192+.

21. Brad Steiger in *Returning from the Light,* p 191+.

22. This account can be followed up in this book, ibid. pp 112-125.

23. The wish to torture others for no apparent reason often goes back a long way, and is usually rooted in past lives. People seem to keep coming back together, in order to transform their unloving behaviour into love. It is possible that Master Gustav experienced similar treatment at the hands of Theuer, who is now returning it to him. Gustav may be taking revenge on his apprentice, because Theuer may have caused him great

physical pain or loss of dignity in a former life.

24. Helen Wambach has published two paperbacks, in which she writes about her research. These can be found in the Literary Index.

25. This quotation can be found in Brad Steiger's book *You will Live again*, p 23. One of the chapters is a summery of Bridey Murphy's case (p 12+). Should you wish to explore this case in greater depth, I suggest reading a book by her hypnotist Morey Bernstein called *The Search for Bridey Murphy*.

26. This quotation was taken from the book *More Lives than One*, by Jeffrey Iverson p16. The entire story about the massacre of Jews in York can be found on pp 30- 46.

27. This account can be found in Jeanne Avery's book *A Soul's Journey*, p140+.

28. This last statement by Dr. Goldberg can be found on p 15 of his book *The search for Grace*.

29. Stevenson in *Children who remember previous Lives – Introduction*.

30. Stevenson in *Where Reincarnation and Biology intersect*, p 2. Next to my appendix scar I have a wart-like birthmark measuring approximately 7mm in length. During regression therapy with a qualified regression therapist, whom I personally trained, I discovered that when I was a French Huguenot named Charles de Puy in 1576, I was stabbed with a knife in exactly that part of my body. After that I had my throat slit. I believe that every

birthmark tells a story, and we are never born with one accidentally. In the future many research scientists will certainly study this phenomenon of birthmarks.

31. Stevenson, ibid. p 12.

32. Stevenson and his colleague Daw Hnin Aye suggest that the person thrown into the well could not have been dead; otherwise, how could he have overheard the conversation of the three men? Clients who have been into regression frequently tell me that after death, especially after a murder, it is common to leave the body and still be able to watch everything from above. In that space they claim to be able to follow conversations and even read the thoughts of those present. As you can see there is much left for the scientists to unravel.

33. This case is clearly portrayed in Stevenson's Thesis, pp 1553- 1565.

34. Stevenson, ibid. pp 1236- 1250.

35. Stevenson, ibid. pp 1382- 1403.

36. Stevenson, ibid. pp 1782- 1801.

37. If you wish to know and understand more about the spiritual laws of life on Earth, I suggest you read my four Novels in seven colors (so far only in German): *Molar, Lilia, Jedem das Seine, (To each his own.* Not available in Germany), and *Maria.* Life in Germany during and after the Second World War is presented in a complete unusual manner. *Molar* in its seven colors can be read

in the complete German version on internet www.trutzhardo.com. Some chapters are translated into English too. And on the same website you find more informations in English. mail@trutzhardo.de.

LITERARY INDEX

Jeanne Avary: A Souls Journey./Austin, Texas 1996.

Morey Bernstein: The Search for Bridey Murphy./New York 1956.

Sue Carpenter: Past lives – True Stories of Reincarnation./London 1995.

Jenny Cockell: Yesterday's Children./London 1995.

Yonassan Gershom: From Ashes to Healing./Virginia 1996.

Bruce Goldberg: Past Lives – Future Lives./New York 1988.

Bruce Goldberg: The Search for Grace./St. Paul, Minnesota 1997.

Trutz Hardo: Entdecke Deine Früheren Leben. (Discover your past lives.) Munich 1997.

Trutz Hardo: Das Grosse Buch der Reinkarnation—Heilung durch Rückführung. (The Big Book of Reincarnation – Healing through Regression.)/Munich 1998.

Jeffrey Iverson: More Lives Than One./London 1976.

Jeffrey Iverson: In Search of the Dead./San Francisco 1992.

Frederick Lenz: Lifetimes – True Accounts of Reincarnation./New York 1997.

Sture Lönnerstrand: I Have Lived Before./Stockholm 1994.

Satwant Pasricha: Claims of Reincarnation. – An empirical study of cases in India./New Delhi 1990.

Tag Powell: ESP for Children. – How to develop your child's psychic abilities./Lago, Florida 1993.

Dick Sutphen: You were Born to be Together./New York 1976.

Brad Steiger: You Will Live Again. (New edition) Nevada City, CA. 1996.

Brad Steiger: Returning from the Light./New York 1996.

Ian Stevenson: Twenty cases suggestive of Reincarnation. / Virginia 1966-1974.

Ian Stevenson: Children who remember Past Lives. /Virginia 1987.

Ian Stevenson: Reincarnation and Biology. – A contribution to the Ethiology of Birthmarks and Birth defects. /West

Port, Connecticut 1997.

Ian Stevenson: Where Reincarnation and Biology intersect. / West Port, Connecticut 1997.

Helen Wambach: Life before Life./New York 1979.

Helen Wambach: Reliving Past Lives./New York 1978.

Ian Wilson: Reincarnation?/Harmandsworth, England 1982.

JAICO PUBLISHING HOUSE

Elevate Your Life. Transform Your World.

ESTABLISHED IN 1946, Jaico Publishing House is home to world-transforming authors such as Sri Sri Paramahansa Yogananda, Osho, the Dalai Lama, Sri Sri Ravi Shankar, Sadhguru, Robin Sharma, Deepak Chopra, Jack Canfield, Eknath Easwaran, Devdutt Pattanaik, Khushwant Singh, John Maxwell, Brian Tracy, and Stephen Hawking.

Our late founder Mr. Jaman Shah first established Jaico as a book distribution company. Sensing that independence was around the corner, he aptly named his company Jaico ('Jai' means victory in Hindi). In order to service the significant demand for affordable books in a developing nation, Mr. Shah initiated Jaico's own publications. Jaico was India's first publisher of paperback books in the English language.

While self-help, religion and philosophy, mind/body/spirit, and business titles form the cornerstone of our non-fiction list, we publish an exciting range of travel, current affairs, biography, and popular science books as well. Our renewed focus on popular fiction is evident in our new titles by a host of fresh young talent from India and abroad. Jaico's recently established translations division translates selected English content into nine regional languages.

Jaico distributes its own titles. With its headquarters in Mumbai, Jaico has branches in Ahmedabad, Bangalore, Chennai, Delhi, Hyderabad, and Kolkata.

SINCE 1946